MW00763948

TREASURES from the ATTIC of the HEART

Susan Garner Moore

Dedication

To my late husband Shields and to our family,
You are such a part of my treasured memories.
Thank you. I love you very much.

Acknowledgements

To God for His wonderful gift of memory. To my family and friends who over the years have helped to create these treasured memories I have tucked away in the attic of my heart, to the Writer/Reader Group at Five Towns for their encouragement to write them in a book, to Jon Michael Miller, the leader of the group, for putting it all together, and to Martin Crabtree for helping to navigate me through using the computer in areas that were new to me. Thank you! Thank you! Thank you!

And

To you, the Reader. May you be encouraged, and perhaps challenged to write your own treasured memories. Enjoy your journey.

Contents

INTRODUCTION

One of the most wonderful gifts God has ever given us is the gift of memory; the ability to tuck away in our lives those moments that brought us happiness, taught us lessons, made us laugh, and put a song in our heart. Do you remember your first day in school, graduation from high school, your first dance, your first kiss? Your first job? What about your wedding? The cry of your first child? Or that special rainbow you saw on a bad day you were having? And on and on....

A long time ago as I sat on the beach at Sanibel Island I began to list memories I never wanted to forget. I was amazed. I thought about the places we had lived, times with my children and my grandchildren, and even the friends I had when I was a child.

There is no special order to memories. Sometimes it is a song we hear, a smell, or something we see, and suddenly the memory pops up. In a moment, we are back in another time. We are there. Perhaps we smile or laugh or even cry, but we remember.

What about the hard times? The hurtful times? The sad times? Those memories are there, too. We remember how we reacted, what we learned, and how we have been able to help others who experienced those rough times.

Treasures from the Attic of the Heart is my story, my memories. I want to share them with my family. I want to share them with you. Perhaps you will begin your own journey, your own adventure into the past. Look back and find your special memories and share them with those you love. Enjoy the trip.

STORIES

The Lonely Tree

Many years ago in Africa, there was a great forest of trees. They were tall and beautiful. Each morning they stretched their limbs toward the sky. They swayed and held their branches even higher. The wind rustling through the forest seemed to chant, "Reach for the sky. Reach for the sky."

Close to the edge of the forest, a little tree sprang up. He wanted to be like the tall trees in the forest. He wanted to reach for the sky. Each morning he stretched his limbs, but as hard as he tried, his limbs would not reach for the sky. Instead, they stretched out to the sides. He was growing out, not up.

Now the tall trees watched as the little one grew. "He is different," one of them said.

"Yes," said another, "he does not belong next to us."

"Look at his funny limbs," said the tallest tree.

The trees talked it over among themselves and decided they would pretend the little tree wasn't there at all. And that is just what they did.

The little tree wanted to be like the other trees but he wasn't. He never would be. A sadness filled his heart and he was lonely.

Time passed and one day the little tree saw a great cloud of dust. It came closer and closer. Soon he saw trucks. Then he saw men. Soon the air was filled with the loudest noise the little tree had ever heard. One by one the tall trees fell to the ground and were carried away on the trucks. It was dark when the last truck pulled away. The little tree heard one of the men say what fine braces for the gold mines, the trees would make.

The moon rose and what the little tree saw made him feel even sadder and lonelier than before. All the tall trees were gone. As far as he could see there was only flat, dusty land. He was truly all alone.

The little tree continued to grow. He grew bigger and his limbs spread further and further to the sides. Small clusters of fruit were scattered among his branches. Sometimes birds came and ate the fruit. Once, a lion rested in his shade and another time two zebras stopped.

One day he saw something moving. He watched as it came closer and closer. He wandered if he was to be cut down and taken away, as the tall trees had been. To his surprise he saw it was a small boy. The boy looked hot and tired, and the tree wondered where he was going. Soon the boy sat down beneath the little tree's spreading limbs, ate some of the clusters of fruit, and fell asleep in the shade. When he woke up he said, "Thank you, little tree. You have given me food and kept me from the hot sun. You are like my grandmother's big umbrella. I shall call you the umbrella tree." The little tree did not feel quite so sad or lonely.

"I must go now," said the boy, "but I will be back." He took some of the fruit in his pocket and waved goodbye. The little tree watched as long as he could.

Many days passed and the tree wondered when the boy would return. Then one day he saw a cloud of dust moving in his direction. As it moved nearer, he saw the little boy. Many people were with him. Soon everyone was sitting under his limbs and sharing his fruit.

"This is my tribe," said the boy, "and they have come to thank you for saving my life. I will one day be the chief of my tribe. We have kept the seeds from your fruit. We will plant them all across this dusty land. Then when they grow big like you, they will be for others, what you have been for me. You will be my special tree and I will visit you each time I pass this way."

As the boy and his tribe disappeared the way they had come, the little tree spread his limbs a little further to the sides. He thanked God for making him the way He did. "If my limbs had reached to the sky like the tall trees, I could never have helped the little boy. Now there will be trees just like me all across this dusty land.

And ... there are.

~

A Fable for Lovers

Once upon a time in the Kingdom of Trees, lived a beautiful princess and a handsome prince. They loved each other very much and wanted to be married. So as was the custom in the Kingdom of Trees, they went to the wise old oak tree to ask him to marry them.

The wise old oak looked at the lovers. "before I can marry you," he said, "you must walk through the forest. When you return, if you still wish to marry, I will marry you."

The prince and the princess quickly agreed and started through the forest. There were flowers everywhere and a gentle breeze blew and birds sang. It seemed as though the whole forest welcomed the young couple.

As they continued on their way, there were less flowers, and fewer birds sang in the trees. The path became rocky and more difficult, and they wondered what had become of the path they had first traveled.

Rain began to fall. The handsome prince found shelter under some low hanging branches and covered the princess with his cloak. The two talked of their adventure, of how beautiful the flowers had been and how difficult the path had now become, almost before they had realized it—and they wondered what lay ahead.

When the rain ended, they found the path. Sometimes sunshine broke through the trees and shown on the lovers and sometimes dark shadows danced around them. They stopped from time to time to watch forest animals at play, and they laughed together—and their laughter filled the forest.

Suddenly, without warning, the prince tripped on a large root and fell to the ground, cutting his head on a rock. The princess quickly tore a piece from her skirt and placed it on the cut. She helped the prince to his feet. "Come and sit over here and rest awhile," she said. All afternoon the princess watched over her prince. She remembered a stream they had crossed and hurried to it and returned with a little water for the prince to drink. "Rest here," she said, "and we will go on tomorrow."

Night fell. "It is very dark," said the princess, "and I am afraid."

The prince drew her closer. "I will take care of you," he said, and she was soon fast asleep.

Morning came. The two awakened. There was no breakfast waiting for them as there was in the castles where they lived. AND, as all folks know, empty stomachs can make for unkind words, hastily spoken.

"I am hungry," said the prince. "Will this path never end?

"Well, if you had not tripped and fallen," replied the princess, "we might have been out of this forest." A mournful breeze rustled the leaves of the trees. It seemed to say "Shoo—Shoo." The prince and the princess looked at each other. "I am so sorry," he said. "So am I," said the princess.

As the path continued to wind through the forest, the couple saw two tall trees surrounded by little saplings. The trees seemed to be watching over the little ones, helping them to grow tall and straight.

"Look," said the princess as they walked through an area filled with the tallest trees she had ever seen. "How strange," said the prince. "Some are broken in half." Just then great gusts of wind blew and the tall trees leaned with each gust and then returned to stand tall once more. As the wind settled back to a gentle breeze it seemed to say, "Bend—Bend."

Sometimes the path was very narrow and hard to follow. "Are we lost?" asked the princess. "No," said the prince, "just trust me."

Sometimes the prince grew weary. "Just a little further," encouraged the princess.

A large broken limb lay across their path. As they walked around it, they saw old gnarled trees hung heavy with gray moss. There was a beauty and contentment about the old trees, and the prince and princess looked at each other and smiled.

Suddenly, almost as quickly as they had entered the forest they were out—and there before them was the wise, old oak. "We are back. Now will you marry us?"

"First, said the wise, old oak, "tell me what you have learned in the forest."

The prince looked deep into the eyes of his beautiful princess. "First, we have learned to enjoy what each day brings—and to care for one another. We have also learned that trouble and change come. But if we hold to one another, we can weather anything—and that kind words and encouragement and laughter lighten the load. And that 'I'm sorry' are words spoken from the heart. And we learned that each stage of life has its own beauty."

"You have learned well," said the wise old oak. He married the handsome prince and the beautiful princess, and they lived happily ever after, remembering what they had learned in the forest.

~

The Most Precious Treasure

Written for Amy Moore for her 30th birthday.

Long ago in a land far away lived a very rich King and his daughter. The King loved beautiful priceless treasures. Each day he went to the secret room where he kept his treasures. He opened a chest of rubies and diamonds and gathered them up in his hands and played with them. He had masterpieces from artists around the world and he stood and gazed at them. There were furs and fine silks and rare sculptures. There were crowns and jeweled swords and everything you could imagine ... and they all belong to the King. He stayed until the sun went down and then he had dinner with his daughter.

When the King went into his treasure room, his daughter gathered her basket and hurried to the poor village at the foot of the mountain. She smiled and waved to the villagers, who waved and smiled back. First, she visited in each house where someone was sick. From her basket, she took medicine and bandages and food to help them get well. Sometimes she visited with the women and took cloth and needles and thread so they could make clothes for their children, or brought seeds for the men to plant their gardens. Always she played with the children, and sang with them, and told them wonderful stores. Everyone loved the princess and she loved them, too. Day after day she visited and returned to the castle as the sun went down.

One night the King looked very unhappy at dinner. "Father," said the Princess, you look unhappy. What is the matter?"

"Oh," said the King, "I need new treasures. Treasures that are more special than the old ones I have." He thought for a while. Then he smiled. "I will send all the young men on a quest to find the most precious treasure in all the world. The one who brings me the one I like the best will receive my chest of diamonds and rubies. All the others may keep their treasure."

Soon many young men set off to find the most precious treasure. One found a black pearl, another found a golden suit of armor, and still another found a rare bird that sang each evening as the sun set. There was a robe of butterfly wings, and a jar of perfume that the fairies had made, and a silver shell that when you put it to your ear you could hear the ocean sing. So many treasures, surely the King would have a hard time deciding which to choose.

The day came when all the young men appeared before the King to present their treasures. "Surely the King will choose mine," each thought. The King said, "ooh and ahh" as each was presented. "How magnificent, such beauty. I can hardly believe my eyes."

As the last young man bowed before the King, the King said, "What treasure have you brought me?"

The young man bowed again. "I have brought you no treasure."

The King was furious. "What do you mean, you have brought me no treasure?"

"I have brought you no treasure because you already have the most precious treasure of all!"

"And what is that?" asked the King.

"The most precious treasure you have is your lovely daughter, the Princess Amy. I have watched her work among the people of the village, loving the children and bringing joy wherever she goes. She has represented you well."

Tears fell from the King's eyes. "You are right," he said. "Amy is my most precious treasure." He thanked the young man and hugged his daughter and told her how much he loved her.

All the young men were given the treasures hey had brought to the King, and a bag of diamonds and rubies. And what about the young man who brought nothing? Well, on the next full moon he married the most precious treasure, Princess Amy. Over the years they had three little boys and they lived happily ever after.

Note: You are a precious treasure to our family and we love you very much. Happy 30th Birthday. The best is yet to come.

~

Charles City Days

In January 1960, my husband graduated from New Orleans Baptist Seminary and we headed for his first pastorate. We had visited the church in view of a call a little earlier and were so happy Mr. Pleasant Baptist Church had decided to call him as their pastor. The church was way out in the country about half way between Richmond and Williamsburg, Virginia – not on a major highway but a small twisting road. The parsonage was an old two-story wood house on a hill with three big oaks in the yard. When we pulled up, folks were there to greet us and help us move in. We could not have asked for more wonderful, caring people.

The house had a porch, a large living room, dining room, breakfast area, bathroom, kitchen and back porch. Upstairs there were three bedrooms. The floors were made of wide boards. Every morning I swept at least a cup of sand out of the house because the boards didn't quite fit together right. One day as I was doing this, a man from the church came by.

"Where'd all this sand come from?" he asked.

"It blew in between the boards," I answered.

Frowning, he said, simply, "No more."

He left and returned later with a truckload of cement blocks and cement and closed the entire lower area of the house. No more sand.

The breakfast area had been enclosed by a former pastor. Having once been a porch, the floor was slanted. One day Uncle Charlie was visiting and wanted a boiled egg for breakfast. I fixed one but when I placed his plate on the table the egg rolled off onto the floor and I chased it down. I loved that house. I loved our time at Mr. Pleasant and could have spent the rest of my life there. Another memory from the breakfast area: We kept a world map on the wall, and each day we prayed for the missionaries and marked the place they served on the map. We were hoping someday to be missionaries, too.

It was winter when we moved in. The church gave us an old fashioned pounding that filled the pantry with home canned goodies. The morning after, we woke up to find God had pounded us with our first snowfall. It was beautiful. Everything was covered in snow and it was still coming down. God is so good and He knows what we need. I'm from Florida and everything is always green. Here everything looked dead until the snow came. Spring would come but I had never seen the change of seasons.

We could see four houses from where we lived. The neighbors on our left gave us a pig. Keep in mind we had never lived in the country. We named the pig Myrtle and kept reminding ourselves we were raising her to eat. Shields built a pig pen not far from the house (we later learned not far enough). As Myrtle grew she liked visiting the neighbors. When the phone rang, it was usually someone calling for me to come and get her. We found the only way she would come was for us to spread a bread trail back to the pen. Some mornings we'd wake up to find Myrtle sitting on our back steps waiting for breakfast. She was one of the family. We also had chickens. The chickens would eat only pig food, and Myrtle would eat only chicken food. I am sure our neighbors had lots of good laughs off us.

When it was time to kill the pig, a man in a truck drove up. "I'm a member of your church," he said. "I don't come to the service, but I always kill the pig." He shot Myrtle and drove off.

There we were with a big dead pig. We did the only thing we knew to do – dragged her into the house and put her in the bathtub. About that time another truck drove up. A man and a woman jumped out, and the woman said, "We're members of your church; we never attend but we always cut up the pig." And sure enough, they did just that.

"Do you want the pig feet?" the man asked. "How about the chitlins"? (We didn't even know what chitlins were.) "How do you want the pig cut up?"

"You take the pig feet and chitlins," Shields said, "and cut up the pig the way you think is best."

We learned that the little building in our back yard was a smoke house and that's where hams and bacon were taken. We had sausage and chops and roasts; things we had never been able to afford going to Seminary. We cooked the fat down and made the lard we would cook with. While the huge pan of lard was cooling on the back porch, Marci got in it. Thank God it had cooled enough she didn't get burned, but cleaning her up was another story. As the year passed each time we had pork, Mark and Marci would say, "Myrtle sure tastes good."

We heated the house with a tall coal stove in the dining room and potbellied stoves in the living room and kitchen. At one time there had been coal stoves in both bedrooms upstairs. One especially cold night, Shields filled the coal stove to the brim so it would last all night. We were all fast asleep upstairs when we heard a loud explosion. Shields and I sat straight up in bed. The cap that covered the hole where a stove used to be was lying on our bed and we were covered in soot and ash. I ran to the kids' room and Shields headed downstairs. The cap was missing from their wall, and Mark and Marci were covered with soot. I rushed down to check on Shields. The stove he had piled full of coal had blown its heavy lid. What a mess! The room was warm and toasty, but a bit blacker than when we went to bed. Not to mention, we could have had a house on fire. God had looked after us.

"Let's go back to bed," Shields said. "Clean up can wait till tomorrow."

We later learned you have to "bank" the coal.

The potbellied stove in the living room was another story. It took wood and was easy to manage ... that is, until the day Shields decided he could recharge flashlight batteries on top of it. It looked like it might work until we heard an explosion. The batteries had blown up. The ceiling above the stove was full of stalactites (or is it stalagmites?). We didn't do that again. I don't remember what I said to the lady who came in while I was cleaning it up.

Our dining room was so big that in the winter when it was too cold for the kids to go outside, we brought the swing set in from the yard and stored it there.

When Marvin was a baby his hips were turned in, and to correct it he wore shoes that looked like they were on the wrong feet. Many is the time we were stopped on the street and someone would say, "Do you realize your child's shoes are on the wrong feet?"

"Thank you," we said, smiling on our way.

At night, he wore a twelve-inch metal bar attached to the shoes. Sleeping in the crib didn't work too well because the bar got stuck in the bed rails. Enter the bunk bed. We had to place him in a bunk bed much earlier than we would have liked. One night we awakened from a sound sleep to hear Marvin crying. I ran to his room and he wasn't there. I heard his cry again and ran downstairs. There he was sitting in the middle of the living room floor. We had taught him how to go down the stairs with the brace, but we never dreamed he'd try it alone and in the dark. I guess once was enough for him because he never did it again.

When we were expecting our fourth child, Marci let everyone know she wanted a girl. Two brothers were enough. Well, Paul was born and she loved him just like she had loved Marvin when he was born. One day I found her kneeling down by Paul's bed praying.

"Please, God, change him into a girl."

Shields had quite a reputation as a bee keeper. When someone had a problem with bees they would call him. We even had our own hive. Shields had ordered it from Sears and Roebuck. We all enjoyed the honey and the honeycomb. One day Marvin, just a toddler, managed to get out to the beehive and sat down at the entrance. When I saw him, the bees were flying in and out, and Marvin was laughing. I called him to come back to the house. He did. The bees never bothered him. They might have been hoping he'd come for another visit. No chance.

We had our first experience with farming. We had a big area where someone had once had a garden. Shields tied a manual plow around his waist and furrowed the rows, not an easy job. One time someone loaned him a mule to plow with. That was a challenge. Sometimes the mule went faster than he did, and sometimes the mule hardly moved. How do you push a mule? You don't. The food from the garden was wonderful: corn, string beans, squash, tomatoes and lots more. Our neighbors showed us how to can food and store it for winter. We only went to the store about once a month. We were doing the canning thing so well we decided to can potato soup. No one told us you can't can potato soup, so we canned 100 quarts and put them in our walk-in pantry. Sometime later when we were asleep (why do these things always happen at night?), we heard Pow! Pow! Pow! We tore downstairs and as the pows continued we realized they were coming from the pantry. We opened the door and found spoiled potato soup everywhere. The smell was terrible and the pows continued. Later when the small explosions had subsided we cleaned up the mess. I wondered why we always seemed to learn country life the hard way. Trust me; we never canned potato soup again.

Another lesson we learned about country living was not to let the kids go out to play or hang wash on the line the first day of hunting season. Not all hunters are created equal.

The men at the church were great about introducing Shields to new things. One night they took him frogging. In the country, you don't use a gig. When you spot a frog with your flashlight, you grab him with your hand and throw him in a burlap bag. They had a good night, and Shields brought home lots of frogs. The next morning, he skinned them as Marci watched. After a few minutes, she ran into the house to tell me, "Daddy is taking the pants off the frogs."

I asked someone at the church how to cook frog legs. "You fry them," she said, "but be sure to stand way back from the stove 'cause them legs can jump right out the pan." I got the frog legs all ready, heated the lard, got the longest fork I had, popped the legs into the pan and stood as far away as I could. No legs jumped out of the pan; not even when I ventured close enough to turn them. They were delicious.

"Did them thar frog legs jump out of the pan?" the church lady "instructor" asked later with a sly grin.

"Not a one," I answered.

One day another lady from the church came by and brought us a dressed" possum to cook. She gave me all the cooking guidelines. I had never cooked a possum but decided it would be another experience. I did just what she said. It smelled horrible and no one would touch it. I threw it down the "back forty" and prayed for what to say to the lady if she asked me at church the next day how the possum worked out. "Lord," I prayed, "if I see the lady let her ask me if I cooked the possum, not if I ate the possum." Sure enough the next morning she headed toward me and I prayed real fast again.

"Did you cook the possum?" she asked.

God is good and answers prayer. "I certainly did," I answered, hurrying off to my Sunday school class.

Yes, there were snakes in Virginia, more specifically in our yard. You know my feelings about snakes. The only good one is a dead one. All our rooms had big windows, and I could spy a snake before it got too close. The first encounter came in the garden. That wasn't too bad. I just stayed out of there. But the second one came when a friend was visiting. This snake was brazen, and came near us. Shields ran for the hoe but out friend had a more innovative idea. She got a burlap sack from her car and caught the snake.

"I want this varmint for my garden to keep the rodents out."

She threw the sack in the back seat of her car and headed home. Bad idea. A short way down the road the "varmint" got out of the sack and slithered near her gas pedal. She let out a squeal, skidded the car to a stop, grabbed the snake and threw it back into the bag. I bet she never forgot that encounter.

Dr. Howard was our doctor, the only one for two entire counties. He was young, married, with five children. Everyone loved Doc. He was a member of our church. My first experience with him was when I ran a hoe in the bottom of my foot. I cleaned it up but a few days later I had a bright red foot and a streak up my leg. Doc gave me a shot and solemnly said, "I think your foot will be okay if you don't lose it." As time passed, I learned that was part of Doc's wonderful sense of humor. Fortunately, I didn't lose my foot.

Doc loved Christmas. Every year he bought one set of gifts for his children and the same set for a poor family also with five kids. He dressed like Santa and delivered the toys after midnight. He also decorated a huge tree near his office, along with a manger, live animals and music. One year we were having out Christmas party at the church when we heard a siren and saw flashing lights as in ambulance pulled up and two paramedics ran in with a stretcher. They pulled back the sheet and there was Doc dressed like Santa with gifts for all the children.

I am a Christmas person. I get that from my Pampa. Anyway, now that we lived in the country we could go out in the woods and cut our own tree. We usually picked it out in the summer. In early December Shields would go out and cut it and bring it home. It had looked small beside the other trees, but it was the perfect size for our home. When we tried to stand it up inside, we couldn't. I was always amazed how much we had to cut off the bottom to make it fit. Most of our decorations were homemade – colorful chains and bits of origami, berry strings and popcorn ropes. We loved it and so did the church. Just before Christmas we invited the church members to come by for cookies and punch and coffee. The kids and I made cookies for weeks and put them in the freezer to get ready.

One day Shields came home with two baby possums. The mother possum had been killed on the road. One of the babies didn't make it. The other one we named Peggy. She lived on our back porch. Every day we let her out to play, and she would come back. One day after she had grown quite large she went out to play and never returned. We figured she met another possum and they decided to start their own family. We missed Peggy. A few years later when we were called to a new church, the freezer, which had always been on the back porch, was moved, and there underneath were all the bits and pieces of chicken bones Peggy had hidden.

We had two cherry trees in our side yard. I never wondered where the children were in cherry season. They were up in the trees. We made wonderful preserves from the cherries that were left. We had grape vines, too. The first year we had a great harvest. When it was over, no one told us you had to cut the vines back until they screamed or you wouldn't have much fruit the next year. Well, our vines didn't scream, and the next year we had luscious vines but not a single grape. We learned, and the third year our vines were loaded. The children liked that because when cherry season was over and the trees no longer held a treasure for them, the grape vines did. I am so thankful our children had some of their young years in the country.

We had an artisan well. The water was incredibly good, and people came from all over the area to get it. It took some effort to work that pump, but it was worth it, just ask anyone. Thank goodness we were somehow connected so we had water in the house.

One of our church families invited our family to dinner. They said they were having chicken. When we got to the table, the meat didn't look like chicken. It was black and cut in small pieces. With a big smile, our hostess said, "I changed my mind. Instead of chicken we're having "rat." We must have looked a bit shocked, so she said, "It's muskrat and we catch them ourselves off the dock." I guess muskrat is a real treat and our friends took big helpings. I ate some, but Shields said he wasn't hungry. It was good but it definitely wasn't chicken.

Shields started visiting the men of the church at the places where they worked. I guess even then a workplace chaplaincy was being born in his heart. He spent a day with a farmer in his barn, made rounds with Doc and spent time with a brick mason. He also went with the local sheriff and heard tales of moonshine stills. The sheriff had gotten a bit too old to run down moonshiners but he worked with younger officers who did the chasing and sometimes ran them right into the arms of the sheriff. The tip off to new stills was who was buying huge amounts of sugar. You can't make whiskey without lots of sugar. One time Shields was out hunting and found an old beat up still. Chalk one up for the law-abiding.

Shields did some hunting. Most of the folks hunted with rifles and shotguns, but Shields was a bow-and-arrow guy. The Garfield's, a family in our church, had given him permission to hunt on their land. I was always concerned when he headed out. He hunted alone, said he was safe because he was on private land. I always wondered about that. There were no fences, so how did hunters out in the middle of the woods know whose land they were on. Shields perched up in a tree and waited for a deer to come by. He never came home with a deer, but I always thought it wasn't that he couldn't have killed one; he just didn't want to. Shields enjoyed his days in the woods.

Mr. Fowler owned one of the two little country stores near our home. He was a character. He loved to visit us. One day he showed up with two rabbits to fix for dinner. He had shot them in the woods. What he didn't tell me was he had used a shotgun and those two rabbits were full of buckshot. That was a new experience. Shields skinned them, and I cut them up and picked out the shot. Sometimes he brought squirrels to cook. Same story: skin, cut up and pick out the pellets. Sometimes I fried the rabbits. They tasted like chicken. Sometimes I made rabbit and gravy. Squirrels made great stew. When Mr. Fowler brought squirrels and rabbits, it was understood he would be back for dinner. He had an alcohol problem and sometimes disappeared for days. When he was ready to come back, he called Shields to come and get him. One time he shared with Shields that before he bought whiskey he drank all the vanilla, lemon and almond extract in his store.

Winnie Bee Orange lived down the road from us. She had a two-story white wood house with a big porch ... and ... a wonderful swing. Her mother was ill and had to stay in bed. Mark and Marci (and later Marvin) and I would walk down to visit her. We said hello to her mother and then went out and sat in the swing, visiting with Winnie Bee. She told us stories about the old days and we told her what was happening at the church. She had beautiful dahlias in her yard. Once she let me pick an armful and we arranged them in a vase for the country flower arranging contest. As the judges looked at them, they made their criticism. According to the experts, we hadn't done anything right. We didn't win a ribbon. What the judges didn't know was that a young pastor's wife and a wonderful older woman who got precious little time outside, had formed a bond that would last for years. It all started with an armful of dahlia. Many years later Winnie Bee died. In her will she left me her silver and china and a crocheted bedspread, and a tatted tablecloth she had made for her hope chest when she was just sixteen years old. The bedspread has been on a bed in our home ever since as a beautiful reminder of a special friend, a woman who was like a mother to me and a grandmother to our children.

Shields built a small swimming pool for the kids. (Yes, it does get very hot in Virginia.) Mark and Marci and Marvin enjoyed it ... except when Shields used it to hold fish he caught, or the neighbors dropped off some of their excess catch. I have to admit those fish stayed fresh until they were cooked.

One year at Christmas Uncle Gail came to visit. He had not met Aunt Margaret at the time. He bought bricks, Tinker Toys and Lincoln Logs for the children. Now, I am not talking little cans, I'm talking the biggest sets that were made. After the children went to sleep on Christmas Eve, he brought the gifts out. Did he wrap them? No. He and Shields used every brick, every log and every tinker toy and filled the living room with the things they built. In the morning, the kids came downstairs and loved it. When Uncle Gail left, he headed for Germany where he met and married Aunt Margaret.

Shields had several "second" jobs during our four years at Mr. Pleasant. One time he drove the school bus for a year. A couple of girls had a lipstick fight in the back of the bus. Not good. The mothers weren't too happy. Another time he stopped the bus at a store. One kid took all the orders and ran in to buy the candy. No one else was to leave the bus. One day another kid jumped off and wouldn't get back on. His sister was on the bus so she got off and walked him home. It wasn't far. That ended the candy stops. Another time Shields was the night manager in a hotel in Richmond. Mark and Marci liked that because some nights he took them with him. The job Shields had that the family liked best was in a cookie factory. Every night for two months he drove to Richmond. When he returned each morning, he always had a bag of broken cookies. That was a treat. Enter our love for broken cookies.

Having pie for dessert "Virginia style" was new to us. When we went to dinner at someone's home there would always be three or four kinds of pie. We were given a small sliver of each to sample. Then we were given a slice of the one we liked best. Some of my favorite recipes came from those "pie sampling" adventures. I have always said, "Some of the greatest cooks in the world were born in Charles City, Virginia."

One of our neighbors had a dairy. Thanks to him, we always had whipped cream and fresh milk. One day I made dinner (using milk) and a new dessert with a secret ingredient – whipped cream, lots of whipped cream. What a fiasco! After the first bite, we knew the cows had eaten wild onions and passed the taste to their milk and on to us.

The Chicahominee River was not far from the house. One day we all piled into a little boat (I don't know where it came from) and headed downstream. We had heard about the locks but had never seen them. Shields cranked the handle that controlled the lock, and the lock opened and our boat went in. The water slowly left the lock and we were lowered down in the river to continue our trip. To return we had to reverse the process. Another country adventure. Whoever said you had to go to the Panama Canal to experience locks?

Spring was a beautiful time of year. The crocuses were the first flowers to break through the snow, then the daffodils and irises. We had so many different irises. A church member's father developed new iris for sale. He always gave us the misshaped bulbs or the ones that were too small. We never knew what surprises we'd have when the bulbs we planted in the fall, blossomed in the spring. I had heard about the cherry blossoms in Washington, D.C. When our cherry trees bloomed, I knew why people wanted to visit Washington in the spring. The trees were incredible.

Once on a church cleanup day, we found and old, beat up communion set in a drawer. No one seemed interested. We took it home and put it on top of the hutch. We thought someone might see it, want to restore it and place it in the church. And someone did. A lady came by and saw it. She knew all about it and offered to restore it. Today that set is in a glass case in the church. Mt. Pleasant was a wonderful church. It was started in 1776. The first members were two sisters who sat on a bench between two trees. Once a month an itinerant pastor galloped in on his horse and preached to the sisters. Years after we moved on, some trees on the property were being cut down. In two of them the ends of the bench were found. They now have a spot in the museum at the University of Virginia.

Next to the garden was a wild looking area (a perfect place for a snake) that contained the world's must luscious blackberries. Every year Shields mowed an area around the patch so we could pick them. For Mark and Marci and later Marvin, it was a dream come true. The cherries were gone, the grapes were not ready, but now there were blackberries. After time in the patch, came the real challenge. How do you get all the berry stains off three little Moores?

A favorite outing was a trip to the library in Richmond. We made it every month and loaded up with books to last till we went again. The library was a wonderful place. In the children's area, books were everywhere and even the littlest child could crawl around and fine some to look at. On the way home, we stopped at a hamburger shop. We could feed four (sometimes five) of us for $1.00.

Our neighbor raised hunting dogs, beagles. They were black and white. Sometimes they were a little brown. They weren't very big and they sure were cute. One day our neighbor asked of if we'd like a dog. It seems a three-legged one had been born in the last litter and they couldn't sell him. We gladly took him and had our very first dog. It didn't seem to bother him that he only had three legs, and it sure didn't bother us. One of my favorite pictures is of Marci sitting on the back porch steps holding him.

The big oak tree in the front yard was a favorite spot for Mark. He could get up in that tree faster than anyone. Once he broke his leg, not from climbing the tree but from climbing a fence in a friend's yard. He went to the hospital and came home with a full leg cast. Within a week he was back in the tree, and within a few more weeks the cast was wearing thin, and required a new one. The leg healed fine. Later he broke an arm at another friend's house. That ended the tree climbing for about six weeks. But his love for climbing trees never wavered.

Miss Helen Binns had a country store across from the parsonage. You never went behind the counters to pick out anything. You asked Miss Binns and she got it for you. There were tools, hardware, groceries, material and sewing needs, you name it, it was there. Best of all there was a candy counter; the kind you stand on tiptoes and look through a glass and pick out what you like. Miss Binns got it and showed it to you. If you changed your mind and wanted something else, it was okay. Candy cost one penny. There was also a big jar of whole dill pickles. It looked like a glass barrel. I don't know if Miss Binns made the pickles herself, but people loved them. They would come in, order one, and stand around and eat the whole thing. Some folks came in just to get the latest news. Miss Binns knew everything that was going on.

One of the things that never ceased to amaze me was how one of my neighbors cooked on a wood stove. She made the best cakes and biscuits and she never burned anything. She just tossed the wood in and added more as she thought she needed it. She always had a pot of hot water on top of the stove just in case someone wanted a cup of coffee or tea.

Shields told wonderful stories about *Aba-thee-nathy*, a little boy who took trips into space or wherever Shields wanted him to go. Marci and Mark loved the stories. I wish we had written them down.

Another special friend we had was Toki Glascock. She was a lovely young woman from Japan who had married an American serviceman. They had lived in Richmond but were given a hard time because Virginia didn't recognize "mixed" marriages. They moved to our area and our church took them in and loved them. Shields had a chance to help Toki find the Lord. One day she came to the house with a beautiful Japanese doll she had made for me. It was in a glass case. Wherever we moved the case and doll always went along. Though somewhere along the line the case broke, the doll is still a part of our home, another reminder of our wonderful, treasured, Charles City Days.

~

Bob

Let me tell you about Bob. Bob is a young, rather slow blue jay. He is big, with a good wing span, a very short tail and a loud mouth. We first met Bob when he crashed into the front window of our home, knocked himself out, and fell onto the porch. Knowing that we had cats in the neighborhood and not wanting Bob to become just another bird burger, we picked him up and placed him on a wide limb of the maple tree in our front yard. From Bob's point of view, I believe we bonded right then.

The next morning ... no Bob. A little later I was in the kitchen and heard Bob's familiar cry ... as if he was inside the house ... and he was. Somehow, probably with parent bird help, he had flown up to the chimney and fallen in. We got a plastic bag, placed it in the fireplace, opened the draft, and down came Bob, none the worse for wear. We dusted the ash of him and again placed him on the wide tree limb.

The following afternoon, we went out to empty the trash and who should be sitting on the side porch waiting for us ... Bob. We picked him up again. This time we placed him on a small limb of another tree ... bad choice. His claws did not know how to go around a limb, so down he fell. After several more attempts, we settled for putting him on the window sill in the back yard near Shield's computer. Bob was happy. We let him know we were leaving the next morning for a week at Sanibel Island, and he would have to manage the best he could.

When we came home, Bob was sitting on the window sill where we had left him.

Now he lives in the back yard with his mom and dad. He still likes them to feed him, but he is learning to take care of himself. Bob now flies daily to the window sill. Could be he is looking for his 'other parents" ... the ones who walk on two legs?

Many years have passed, but each year our yard is full of blue jays. Shields and I believe they are Bob's children and grandchildren who have heard him tell his stories over and over and have come to see for themselves.

~

A Night I Will Never Forget

One evening the phone rang. It was Clayton.

"What are you doing, Grandma?" he asked.

"Nothing special," I said.

"How about we go to the beach and see the sunset."

It wasn't long and he drove up in the blue truck. We played a game for a while and then we went out to get in the truck. As usual, Clayton opened my door. We drove to Redington Beach, hopped out (after he opened my door), and headed for the water. It was still light and we walked a long way on the beach. We stopped to watch a great blue heron with a hurt wing. As I turned from watching the bird, I saw Clayton writing something in the sand with a golf tee he had found. It said, Grandma and Clayton were here and gave the date. Clayton took a picture of what he had written and a picture on me looking over the water, waiting for the sun to set. We watched until the last bit of the sun disappeared below the water.

Then Clayton said, "We better head back." He opened my door, climbed in, and away we went. Thoughts of that wonderful evening raced through my mind.

When we got back to the house, he turned to me and said, "I'll make some peanut - butter fudge for you." AND He Did. It was delicious. Clayton is the official fudge maker, since his Grandpa, who originally held that title, died.

We played another game and he said, "Grandma, I'd better head home." It was about 10. I gave him a big hug, and watched from the porch as he headed home. A few minutes later the phone rang. It was Clayton calling to say he had gotten home.

I will never forget that evening with Clayton. What he had written in the sand would wash away, but what he had written in my heart would last forever.

I am looking forward to your graduation from Keswick. I'll miss you when you go away to college but I look forward to watching how well you do, and celebrating with you as you begin your new adventure.

God bless you. I love you very much.

~

Clips from the Family Newsletters

As our children grew up and moved away from home, I wanted a way for all of us to keep in touch, to know what we were all doing, our jobs, our friends, our good times and hard times. Sort of like we did around the table when we all lived together. Thus, the Family Newsletter was born. I wrote each week. I wish I had kept a copy of every letter, but I didn't. Here are a few clips from some of them.

September, 1987

Daddy is cleaning the freezer. I think he is making some rare discoveries ... at least that's what it sounds like from his comments ... things like, "Oh gosh, what is this?" or "I don't believe it," or "Where in the world did this come from?" or "Sue, did you mean to put a whole cabbage in here?" (I didn't mean to. It just fell in with the frozen food. Besides, it was a cauliflower, not a cabbage.) All his comments are punctuated by deep sighs. Thank goodness the job is almost done. He just found the remains of last year's turkey and decided it could go

We had birthday dinner for Dad last night. Marci took us to the Brown Derby. They had steak and I had fish. We rented a tape and stretched out to watch *The Little House of Horrors*. It ranks right up there with *The Attack of the Killer Tomatoes*. Steve Martin was good as the dentist and the plant was a marvel. I had read reviews on the movie and it was supposed to be good. The three singers drove us nuts. We hoped the whole time that the plant would have a good meal off of them.

December 1987

Tomorrow Dad has a meeting with the people at the airport to talk about having a chaplain there. His meeting with Florida Power was excellent. Well, I have to tell you about OPERATION DAD. November 30th (Monday) was Dad's big interview. Joel and Marci were here for dinner and about 7:30 we decided at that Dad should have the big overhaul. Keep in mind this was Friday night. So, we left the dishes and headed for the Mall. The salesman was very patient with us as we told him what we wanted for Dad. We watched as Dad modeled suits. He looked great. Then the big tie caper. Joel won out with one that had lots of red; great with the black suit and white-on-white shirt. The salesman didn't even bat an eye when we told him we needed the suit the next day, alterations and all.

Next it was shoe time. The clock was ticking away Nobody in the mall had shoes to fit Dad. At that moment, we wished we could have a Dad with skinny feet instead of wide ones. A new shoe store had opened up next to the tracks so we flew over there. They had three pairs that fit him, and just as the store was closing and after another long deliberation, we selected just the right one. Next day, Saturday, Dad worked but Marci didn't let that stop her. She called and made an appointment for Dad to get his eyes checked for new glasses. While Dad got his exam, we looked for frames. We finally agreed on gold wire (Joel's idea) ones. This was a one- hour service place and we were there at the last hour. They got the glasses ground only to find they had made an error. They told us we would have to wait until tomorrow to get the glasses.

ENTER MARCI ... again.

"Our dad," she said to the salesman, "must them tomorrow morning for an appointment, and the only reason we came here was to get fast service you advertised."

We got the glasses. He looked absolutely perfect. Clothes may not make the man, but they sure help.

February 1990

Well, the big news this week is the demise of Joel's car. The good news is no one was hurt. It seems Joel was thinking of buying a small boat and had gone to pick it up and test-sail it to the Bay Pines boat ramp. A friend brought Joel's car to the ramp and put it in place to attach the boat. With brakes on, the friend got out of the car, left the door open and went to help Joel with the boat. The next thing anyone knew, the car was in six feet of water.

The wrecker who came to pull the car out said that happens a lot at that ramp. Pulling the car filled with that much water really tore up the front of the car. Joel's insurance man is due on Thursday and is expected to total the car. Needless to say, the boat went back to the owner. It may turn out to be a blessing. Joel can pay off the car and use the company van he has been given. No car payment and no car insurance ... that could help anyone's budget.

Paul, guess you will soon be on the high seas and heading for your home port. Enjoy your first "ship ride."
(I don't think "ship ride" is navy talk) I hope the seas will be calm.

July 1990

From our North Carolina/Georgia resort vacation

with Gail and Margaret: Gail and I hiked to three different waterfalls. One of the trails had a sign that read, "Short forty minute walk." We took it. It wasn't forty minutes, it was 45 ... ten minutes straight down and 35 minutes straight up. The sign failed to mention the creeks you had to forge, the trees to be hopped, or the three sets of narrow steps (28 in each ... Gail counted them on the way down so he could remind me on the way back up.)

The falls were beautiful and worth the walk. There were a number of people down there when we arrived. One was an old mountain lady who had brought her grandchildren to see the falls. She was probably in her eighties, maybe older, dressed in a lovely dress and using a cane. There was not a drop of sweat ... not even perspiration on her. As she heard us commenting about the scenery, she sweetly told us there was a "second" way back to the top. She said it was steeper than the one we had taken but that she had taken it many times. From the tone of her voice and the way she held her arm to show us the angle of the trail, we decided it was only for mountain goats and little old mountain ladies.

The next place we stayed had horses. Yes, I rode a horse ... twice. When we ambled up to the corral (that's west Georgia talk) the man asked what experience we had. Dad, Margaret and Gail had horse experience. When the man looked at me, I had to admit that my horse history was limited only to having my picture taken on a pony when I was six and to riding a mule at my Uncle Alf's house. It was the few minutes spent on the mule that qualified me to join the group. I am not sure the leader was totally convinced because he gave me a 21-year-old horse named Boogieman and assured me numerous times that it was as gentle as a lamb. Sure enough, it stuck to the lead horse like glue and never missed a step on the trail. Dad had a spunky horse and rode like he did it every day. Gail's horse wanted to stop every two minutes to eat grass, but it didn't take long for Gail to show him who was the boss. Margaret's horse even did some trotting for her. It was really fun.

Thanks for your calls, Marvin. I love to hear your voice. There is a little laugh in your voice which always adds a sparkle to my day. Lambchop has a special place in the animal basket.

January 1991

I took all the Christmas decorations down last Sunday. That has become a cherished ritual. As I take each ornament off, it is a time to remember the family and friends and events that each represents. The oldest thing on the tree is the corsage I carried on my Bible when Dad and I got married. There are little soldiers Mark got in Germany ... lots of Hallmark ornaments from Marci ... glass ornaments you kids gathered at the dump years ago ... owls and snowflakes that Grandmother Moore made the first year we were back in Tampa ... special ones from Martha and Ralph ... gingerbread men and candy canes we bought the first year we moved into the house ... and on and on. Dad put the tree into its box. I am always amazed how such a big tree fits into such a little box, but Dad does it. I haven't decided if he is magic or if he is the victor after a battle to the death with the tree. Anyway, all is safely tucked away for another year ... or at least ten and a half months. I love Christmas.

November 1991

Paul, you sound great. In his last call he shared an educational fact with us. I think I could have lived without it and it has certainly changed any travel plans I may have had to visit that part of the world. FACT: there are sea snakes in the Persian Gulf ... and they are poison. The Navy instructs its men to cover their ears if they fall overboard. It seems the little rascals have small teeth like coral snakes and they need to chew on soft tissue. Sweetie, please stay out of the water.

Well, I had a unique experience today. I went to a chiropractor for the first time in my whole life.

"I've always been terrified of chiropractors," I told him.

"I understand," he answered, "but we've been given a lot of bad press. Don't worry, we are safe and knowledgeable."

I waited to see. He did do a good exam. Then he put me on this little electric current device (the closest I'll ever come to the electric chair, I hope). For ten minutes this little electric current darted from one side of my back to the other. After the first jolt, when I almost catapulted off the table, it was fine. Then he took me to the next room. There was a strange looking table standing on end. I was instructed to stand against it so he could lower it.

"Does it go down fast or slow," I asked.

"Not fast, not slow."

Before I could blink ... zoom ... I was down. You be the judge. He pushed here and pulled there and gently told me that I would probably be a little sorer when I left, than when I came in. He was right. He suggested some wonderful floor exercises to do at home.

I tried them just now. After today's treatment, it took me a long time to even get down on the floor, and I did what little I could. When I started to get up, I found I was a beached whale. I can't remember how long it took me to get up, but I am in a fully upright position as I write this. Can you believe I am going back tomorrow?

January 1993

I came upon one of the great puzzles of life. How do you put a seven foot Christmas tree back into a 4 x 4 x 2 foot box? Don't suggest to 1) jump on it, 2) hog tie it, 3) wrestle it, or 4) try to disguise it and leave it casually in the corner of the living room. None of the above work. I tried or at least thought of trying all of them. However, I did manage to get the tree back into the box ... with a few adjustments. A metal pole now sticks out of one end, the tip of the tree will forever have a permanent bend, and numerous branches will never know completely what the inside of the box looks like.

I also discovered a new sound. Maybe you have heard it. You have just taped up the tree in its box; you step back to admire your work when suddenly POP. The tape flies off the box and the tree is free. I finally got it in the closet with boxes of Christmas decorations stacked around it ... and the door closed. I have a feeling a "Do not disturb until next Christmas" sign should be hung on the door. But, heck, why spoil someone's fun when sometime in June they open the closet door to be greeted by a jack-in –the box Christmas tree.

November 1993

Speaking of Christmas, I mustered up my courage and opened the "Christmas closet" ... you remember, the one I told you about putting or at least attempting to put the tree, train, wreath, garland and other goodies away in? The one that I threw myself against to close? The one I cautioned everyone to stay away from and not dare to open? It wasn't really courage that caused the early opening ... it was necessity. Our pastor took a church in Texas and his daughter is staying with us until she graduates in June. His wife will be with us for about five weeks ... and they need closet space. The only place for my clothes was ... you guessed it ... the "Christmas closet." Well, I opened the door; nothing happened ... I smiled. I meticulously extracted the first item, a nondescript box. MISTAKE! The entire closet followed. Just as I had feared, the tree had once again succeeded in making good his escape from his box. The train pushed back his lid, the garland catapulted out like a snake testing freedom for the first time, and the wreath I managed to catch just before it rolled out the door. You will be pleased to know I have learned my lesson. I carefully packed all the decorations away in big boxes and stored them under the table in Dad's office. The tree and the train, I casually tossed in the closet in you know who's office. If he or anyone else opens the door, it will look like a disaster but at least it won't be dangerous. Besides, I'll be decorating in a few weeks.

I have some news for you ... if you don't already know ... and you probably may, as I seem to be the last to learn earth shaking bits of news like the one I am about to share. Here goes: The shelf life of a Twinkie is 27 years. That's incredible. Think of the implications. I could go into the store tomorrow and hold in my hand a Twinkie that will outlive me. And if the shelf life is 27 years, how long will it lie in my stomach (should I choose to live dangerously and eat one). When I come to the end of my life, the doctor might say, "She's gone, but we can't kill that Twinkie. Or we might coin a new phrase, "Old Twinkies never die, they just petrify." The possibilities are amazing. I am going to make a trip to the store and check a few dates. Who knows, the Twinkie may come under study as we seek to lengthen our "shelf life" on earth.

June1998

One day after receiving the last Family Newsletter, Marci called in a snake sighting. She and Pam headed out their front door ... there he was, an ominous critter sunning himself. Now, had he been wise, he would have exited stage left as fast as possible ... he didn't. For him the choice of fight or flight was fight. He coiled up, stuck his tongue (which was longer than his body) and swayed menacingly. That was enough for Marci, normally a peaceful, nonviolent, snake-ignoring person. While Pam kept watch, Marci disappeared back into the house and returned equipped to do him in, and she did. Another snake bit the dust. Congratulations, Marci, for a job well done.

November 1998

Aunt Sylvia, so glad you received a break from jury duty and are on the road again. I bet Ralph is glad, too. Thanks again for the storage bag for the Christmas tree. I am sure it will be a new challenge for him. He does so well blasting out of his box.

Well, here's a snake story for the books. It comes from Mark. As he came out of the house the other day, he heard a noise, sort of a cry for help ... the sound of desperation. He looked up in the palm tree and there was a long green snake enjoying breakfast. Protruding from his mouth were the legs

38

of a frog ... the legs still kicking, the snake straining to get the whole frog in his mouth ... not a pretty sight. Now, the interesting thing was the source of the noise. Was it the frog who obviously was not going to get out? Or, was it the snake who was making a do-or-die effort to get the whole frog in? Life in the country is great ... I think. A happy ending for me would have been that the snake was killed, the frog rescued, and life on the pond restored. I grew up on fairy tales and I love an "and they lived happily ever after." PS. Remember my motto: "The only good snake is a dead snake."

You have heard of "Snake Away," thanks to Ann? BUT have you heard of "Sticky Feet"? If raccoons get into your attic (as they did in Joel's) and they are getting in by climbing trees near your house ... this is your lucky day. Simply spread Sticky Feet around the bark of the tree (high enough that little people can't reach it) then when the raccoons come, their feet will get sticky, they won't like it, and they won't return. The gentleman who sold it to Joel said there was one drawback. You might look out your window and see a snake or two stuck to it. Personally I think that is a great selling point.

December 1998

Well, this is the last chapter of the exploding Christmas tree box. After cutting the ten pounds of tape I had wrapped around it, out popped the tree. The box stood gleefully by waiting to be stored away. He loves these after Christmas wrestling matches to get a big tree back in a small box. Most of the times he wins. BUT this year it is different. Since Aunt Sylvia sent the tree bag, the box went. Not quietly, mind you, but he went. I took him out to the garbage can and started stuffing ... he resisted ... I bent him in half ... he popped back. I tried tearing the box apart ... not good. That box had been around so long it was petrified. Finally, I put him in head-first and threw myself on the lid of the can. It worked. I am presuming he was picked up by the trash man; he wasn't there when I put the can away ... but you never know.

~

The Great Valentine

We were still living in Charles City, Virginia. Marci and Mark were both in elementary school. It was Valentine's Day and I wanted to do something special for our children. Then it happened! The Great Valentine was born. When Mark and Marci came in from school and walked into the dining room, there over the table hung a three-foot-tall Great Valentine. He was made of red poster board. He had a big heart for his head, a bigger one for his body, and lots of smaller hearts hung together for arms and legs. There was a glass of milk, a tiny dish of valentine candy, and a red napkin for each of them.

"This is the Great Valentine," I told them, "and he has come to say, Happy Valentine's Day to you." They were so excited. They ate their candy, drank their milk, and played a little while with the Great Valentine. Then they went upstairs to put on their play clothes. When they returned, The Great Valentine was gone.

"Where did he go?" they asked. "Will he come back?"

"He will be back every Valentine's Day."

This was a tradition in our family until the last of our five children graduated from high school. Every year the great Valentine was different. One year he was tiny with a pointed finger like E T. Once when Marci was in college she had a friend who was studying to be a doctor so the great Valentine was twelve inches high, had a paper stethoscope around his neck and carried a little bag. One year he carried a football. If one of the children was involved in a sport, the Great Valentine reflected the sport.

One year Mark was in the Army serving in Germany. I got a letter asking if the Great Valentine knew he was in Germany. I assured Mark he did

After many years with a different appearance every year, a letter arrived from the Great Valentine. It was Valentine's Day and in the evening Shields and I took all the kids to dinner at the Olive Garden. They all talked about the Great Valentine and the ones they liked the best. After dessert, I told them I had a letter to them from The Great Valentine. I opened the letter and read:

Dear Kids,
Happy Valentine's Day.
I have loved being a part of your lives all these years. You have grown into such fine young people. You are very special to me.
After last Valentine's Day, I decided it was time to retire. I moved to one of the South Sea Islands and I am living on the beach. It is great. Thank you for letting me be with you each Valentine's Day. I will miss you.

Love,

The Great Valentine

Now, if you can, picture this: seven adults sitting around a table in the middle of the Olive Garden, laughing and having a great time, when suddenly five of them are crying their eyes out, tears running down their cheeks. Thank goodness for extra napkins on the table.

"Will he ever come back?" one of the boys asked.

"Perhaps he will. but I don't know. I do know he will be a forever memory in our family, to be recalled and enjoyed again and again."

And He is.

~

Little Cat

Once upon a time in the kingdom of cats, a Little Cat was born. There was something special about her. Oh, she meowed and purred and frolicked and played like other kittens, but there was a thoughtfulness and a spirit of adventure about her. Her eyes had a faraway look, like she was seeing something that others didn't see. Sometimes when she sat gazing at the stars, the other kittens would come and sit by her, hoping to see what Little Cat saw

They soon tired of trying and went back to their play, leaving Little Cat to her dreams. Sometimes she would see a blackboard and chalk. Sometimes small white caps surrounded her. Once she saw herself in a room, sitting begins a desk. There was an open door and cats kept coming and going. Little Cat wondered what it was all about.

The years passed and the dreams continued. One day Little Cat told her Daddy and Mother and her Brothers, "I want to go to Cat U; I want to be a nurse cat and help other kittens to have dreams like I have had." Before she left, her Daddy and Mother told her that cats have nine lives and they should use them wisely. Looking back on graduation day, Little Cat was sure she had used at least one life going through three universities.

Little Cat went to work. After some years, she came to Kuttlerville. She taught for a few years and then she became the Head Cat...the Big Feline...the Top Tabby for the Division of Nursing. It was then she remembered the dream she had had when she was a kitten. She had seen herself behind a desk with her door open and big cats and little kittens were coming in to cry, and talk, and get advice. Now here she was. It wasn't a dream. It was all true.

It was not an easy job, but she loved it. There were meetings to chair. One word could be heard loud and clear at faculty meetings – TIME! Little Cat allowed just so much time for each issue. Everything stopped...unless of course, The Faculty Cats wanted more time. And then there was accreditation. The Heavy Cats from the North would sweep in and check things out. So much to do to get ready; so little time. There was curriculum revision, and curriculum revision, and curriculum revision. It was a tense time. The Faculty worked hard, but so did the Little Cat. She wanted everything to be perfect.

The student nurse kittens were Little Cat's first concern. Were they learning what they needed to know? Could they apply what they had learned? Were they safe practitioners? Were those having trouble, getting the help they needed?

The Faculty Cats liked her style. "She is a good listener and fair," said one.

"A real professional", said another.

"She gives good advice, too", said the Persian cat. "She told me, it's ok to be human. No one is perfect. Mistakes happen."

"She taught me how to get organized. I even started making lists like she does," meowed The Tiger Cat.

"Thanks to her, I'm more flexible," purred the Manx Cat.

"I love to watch her negotiate. She says she is still learning, but I think she is super," said the Siamese.

Little Cat's name appeared on five Who's Who lists and she served on numerous boards. There had been many honors but her favorite was the invitation to the White House luncheon on National Nurses Day. She had had her picture taken with the President's wife, who would later be the Mother of a President. Now that is really something to purr about.

The seventeen years had passed quickly. Now it was time for a new plan, a new adventure. Little Cat was ready for a change. There would always be people to love and challenges to be met.

A knock came at the door. "It's time to go to your retirement party", said the Cat who managed the office for her

The room overflowed with friends and colleagues, and everyone clapped when Little Cat walked in. There were hugs and tears. There were "Thank Yous" and "Best Wishes". There were speeches and laughter. Love and warmth were everywhere. Little Cat had given her best- she had left her mark. Kuttlerville was saying "good-bye" to one of its finest, and they knew it.

Tears ran down Little Cat's face as she said good-bye. She remembered what her Daddy and Mother had said about cats having nine lives. She had sent one with her dreams, another getting her education, and a third in her work. Six more to go. A million things rushed through her mind: more time with her Husband, leisurely dinners to enjoy Italian food, reading mysteries and romance novels. Shopping, shopping and more shopping. No one loved finding a bargain more than Little Cat. There would be camping and hiking, balloon races, Shakespeare and the arts, tea parties, and baking and on and on. What lay behind her had been wonderful; what lay ahead of her would be fantastic. Little Cat smiled to herself and secretly thought: GOODBYE KUTTLERVILLE! HELLO WORLD!

~

Sanibel Island

If I had to name my favorite place to visit, it would be Sanibel Island. My husband Shields and I had heard about this beautiful island off the coast of Fort Meyers, Florida.

We loved everything we had heard; especially the fact that there was a camp ground. We had five young children so a decision to camp made the trip affordable. We loaded up our VW van and headed out. The trip didn't take long. Shields parked the van on our campsite and off we headed to investigate the beach.

There weren't many people on the beach. We played in the water, built a sand castle, and collected some awesome shells. We were having the time of our lives. As it grew later, we ran back to the camp ground, took a shower, and got ready for dinner. We cooked on the grill. The food was delicious; it always is when you cook it and eat it outside. We laughed, shared stories with some of the other campers, and before long, realized it was time to hit the sack. All seven of us slept in the VW van. We were tired, happy, and looking forward to tomorrow. As I lay there I realized; I had fallen in love with Sanibel Beach. I wanted to come back.

In the morning, we made one more trip to play at the beach and then packed up the van and headed home. It had been a one night stay but a forever memory.

I have been back many times. When I am there, time stands still. Perhaps I am a child again, a young woman, a mother of five, or perhaps I've reached middle or even old age, whatever. My love for the beach has never faded

In the next few pages, I'd like to share some of my forever memories and the life lessons I have learned over the years, on the beach at Sanibel Island.

This is a morning I'll never forget. I was walking by myself. It was barely light, a breeze was blowing, and I was feeling that same joy I feel every time I walk the beach.

Then I heard a noise that grew louder by the second. I looked around trying to figure out what it was. Then I saw it; an airplane coming around the end of the island, flying very low over the sand and headed right for me. I hit the ground, my face buried in my hands. As the plane flew over me, I got up, still in one piece and covered with sand. I had probably given the pilots their laugh for the day. I learned later that it was the plane that sprayed for mosquitoes.

I laugh now, but it wasn't funny then.

I love collecting shells. Sometimes I am looking for particular shells. A friend had asked me if I would bring her some scallop shells. I assured her there were lots of scallop shells and they were beautiful. I looked for them for half an hour and found only one. I saw a lady who was collecting, too and asked her if she had found any scallop shells. She showed me a bucket full. "Oh," she said, "you are looking in the wrong place." She pointed me back the way I had come and added, "They are beyond that condo. I thanked her, followed her directions, and found the beautiful shells my friend wanted.

As I headed back to share my adventure with Gail, Margaret and my husband Shields, I wondered how many times I had looked for something – happiness, joy, friendship or peace – only to realize I was looking in the wrong place.

Gail and I headed out on our early morning walk along the beach. I looked up at the sky. It was red; very red. "Gail, we'd better not walk right now. You know that old saying, "Red sky in the morning, Sailors take warning."

"I've never been a sailor," Gail said, "and we will be fine."

We walked quite a way, when suddenly the rain came down and the thunder and lightning followed. We dashed for a pier with a small covered area. We weren't alone. I guess they weren't sailors either. We were there a long time. Gail's stomach started growling and he said, "Let's head home. It's time for breakfast."

We took the road back to the condo, rather than the beach. Sometime the rain came and some time the thunder and lightning. We dashed from cover to cover. Finally, we could see our condo. All that separated us was a huge ditch filled with mud and dirty water, and no telling what else.

"We can walk through this," Gail said as he started through.

"Not me," I said.

Gail motioned for me to come. I was not about to walk through that ditch. I made my decision. I backed up as far from the ditch as I could. I needed a good running start to leap across. Believe it or not, I made it and soon we were having breakfast in the condo.

Later that afternoon, I walked back to look at the ditch. Even I was amazed that I had made it across. Needless to say, I never tried that again.

Ever since our adventure, I take seriously, "Red sky in the morning; sailors take warning." I stay inside and read a book.

Today was Friday, Gail's favorite day for treasure hunting. All week long as we walked the beach, he was looking for treasures people had left on the beach. You know, caps, buckets, toys, shirts, whatever. He never picked it up the day he saw it, but if it was still there on Friday, it was his. When I first saw him doing this I thought, "How nice. He is helping to keep the beach clean". I was wrong. He was picking up "treasures" for his collection. Sometimes he might wear a cap or even a shirt he had found. Gail didn't need anything but this was his special game and he loved it.

Gail and Margaret were special friends of ours. I had known Gail since I was about 21. My Grandmother had rented Gail a room in her home when he was in town. He met Shields when Shields and I married. He even visited us in Seminary in New Orleans and in Charles City, Va. Where Shields had his first church.

When we moved to our second church in Rustburg, VA, Gail called us to say he was back from a visit in Germany and had something to show us. He arrived a few days later for us to meet Margaret, his wife, whom he'd met and married in Germany. We loved her. That was the beginning of a friendship I will never forget.

The years passed. In 1970, they began driving to St. Petersburg where we lived. They had two young daughters. The four of them spent one to two weeks with us at Christmas. Later when all the children were grown, we would spend a week in May and a week in August with them in their condo on Sanibel. They still spent Christmas with us and sometimes another week in May.

Gail died a few years before my husband. Margaret has Alzheimer's and is in a lovely assisted living facility on the east coast of Florida near her daughters. I miss our friendship and our times together, but the memories live on in the Attic of my heart.

~

The Stick Horse

Many years ago, I stopped at a huge garage sale. There were so many things to see: dishes, pots and pans, furniture, clothes, books, games and toys, lots of toys. It was when I was looking at the toys, I spied him, a homemade stick horse. His head was made of a blue cotton material with tiny red and white dots and stars all over it. He had big black and white eyes, a small nose, a red floppy mane, and a black ribbon mouth with a smile that seemed to touch his red ears. I picked him up. No matter how I turned him and looked at him, he looked at me. I could almost hear him saying, "Take me home, your grandchildren will love me." I looked at the price tag, seventy-five cents. That was a lot of money twenty years ago, so I put him down and walked away.

When I got home I thought, "I wish I had bought that stick horse."

About two weeks later, I went to a garage sale at a large church and there he was, the stick horse. As I picked him up and smiled, he seemed to say, "What took you so long to come back? You knew you wanted me for the boys." He was still seventy-five cents, but it was and still is the best seventy-five cents I have ever spent. He has galloped through every room in our home, been a baseball bat, a golf club, hockey stick, a band baton, and even a microphone. Of all the toys, I have purchased over the years, none has been loved or enjoyed more.

When the boys were not with us, the stick horse stood tall in the animal basket in the living room waiting for them to return. Even as I share this story, the stick horse is still part of our family. He officially oversees the animal basket and welcomes all the new animals who come to live there.

Our three grandsons, now twenty-three, twenty-one and nineteen come by for a visit when they are in town. It is not unusual for them to walk by the animal basket and pat the stick horse on the head and say something to him, or take him out and walk around with him. Perhaps someday when they marry and have children, the stick horse will move on to bring the same joy and forever memories, to their children.

~

The Jolly Mouse

Once upon a time in the little village of Parkington, there was a factory that was run entirely by mice. Some of the mice were in charge, some taught the young mice to grow to be the best they could be, some helped in the office, and some worked in the lab.

One day a new mouse came to work in the factory. She was assigned to work in the lab. She was jolly, she laughed a lot, and she made the other mice feel good. Mice who had problems came to talk to her. Student mice would come and ask her questions. She was never too busy to listen or help.

The Jolly Mouse liked happy sayings and mystical music, and she was always bringing new things to the factory to share.

She was married to a kind and gentle giant of a mouse. They had moved to Parkington from the mountains in the far north. Winters in their old home had been cold and they longed for a sunny warm place to live. The only problem was, they had left most of their family and friends behind. Sometimes they were lonely and missed the mice back home. One day they planned they would return, but not for a long, long time.

The years passed and the Jolly Mouse settled into her job. Sometimes she shared fun stories about her life growing up on a farm, and some time she shared Mikey Mouse stories.

The other factory mice wondered what made the Jolly Mouse so understanding when they were hurting.

"She always knows just the right things to say," said the mouse whose hero was Mikey Mouse.

"Her hugs are the best in the world," said another.

"She is wonderful," said the dark haired mouse who worked in the office.

"She must never have been touched with sadness," said a new mouse.

"Not so,' said the wise old mouse. "Have you seen the tiny gold heart she wears around her neck?"

"Yes," said the new mouse. "It is very lovely."

"Well, the mice she works with in the lab gave it to her when her tiny baby grand mouse went to live in heaven. She had been very sad and tears had run down her cheek. The tiny heart had said that they loved her and knew she was hurting."

"Then that is the reason she cares so much about us when we are hurting," said the new mouse.

"That is one of the reasons," said the wise old mouse. "When hard things happen in our lives, it should make us better mice to each other. Personally, I have always believed she was made extra special and wherever she goes, she will always spread her own kind of magic.

Then one day it happened. The jolly mouse said she was leaving. The kind and gentle giant mouse had been transferred back to the cold country, not too far from the rest of the family. The news spread quickly through the factory.

"We will miss her very much," said all the mice.

"How do you say goodbye when you don't want someone to leave?" asked a young mouse.

"I think my heart is breaking," sighed a tall mouse.

"We must have a party for her with all our favorite foods. We will laugh and talk, and hug, and remember all the fun times we have had together."

"Try not to cry," said the wise old mouse. "You know how easily she cries, and we do not want this to be a sad time."

"I know the perfect gift for her," whispered one of the mice. "Let's make a waterfall. Each time she sees it she will be reminded of how much she is loved."

"And the sound of the water gently falling on the leaves, will be like our laughter," giggled another.

"When she looks deep into the tiny pool below the leaves, she will see our reflections smiling back at her," said the mouse with red hair. "I like that."

So, day after day they gathered the materials and lovingly worked to create their farewell gift for the Jolly Mouse. When it was completed, they stepped back and looked in wonder at the waterfall.

"It is beautiful, just like our friend," they said.

Over the next few days they filled the waterfall with tears of happiness that had tumbled from their eyes as they remembered special moments they had shared with her.

Finally, just as they planned, the mice held a wonderful party for the Jolly Mouse, and they gave her their special gift to take with her. They wished her well and waved goodbye as she disappeared through the doors of the factory. She was gone from their lives but she would always live on in their hearts.

~

Snake Tales

I am a person who doesn't like snakes. That's a little mild. I'm really afraid of snakes. Terrified might be a better word. Give me a dinosaur, a panther with eyes that glow in the dark of night, anything but a snake.

Why then are these snake stories tucked away in my memory? I'm not sure, but perhaps it is because people sent me their snake tales in hopes I would laugh at their experiences and begin to fear snakes less. It didn't work. I still believe the only good snake is a dead snake.

The snake that crawled up to the window and stared at me while I was on the computer has made a return visit. This time he was bolder. I casually walked out the front door, went to the car, unloaded some bags and headed back in. That is when I saw him. He was between me and the front door ... not good. He wouldn't move ... he just lay there with his head raised up, looking around like he was king of the front porch. I did the natural thing ... I ran to the back door ... it was locked ... I knocked (not really ... I banged and banged) and Shields, my husband, just sat at the computer ... he was on the phone. Now let me ask you, what is more important, talking on the phone or rescuing your wife? For the moment, the phone won. Finally, the door opened and I told my story. Dad said he'd get the broom and chase it away. Not my broom ... who wants a snake broom? He took the mop instead and went to do battle. By then the snake was gone ... nowhere to be found ... hiding out ... waiting for another day to spread terror. This is definitely a job for "snake away." You Richmond folks who sent that precious jug had no idea how much I would use it. Thanks again.

Today while I was at the computer, I casually looked out of the window just in time to see a stick fall to the ground. I was confident it was a stick because it didn't move. A short time later I looked out the window and the stick was gone. Not good. I now realized it was a black snake who hit the ground harder than he planned, was knocked unconscious temporarily, woke up, and moved on to terrorize the neighborhood another day.

Ann, thanks for your snake story. Makes me glad that I don't have a screened porch. Here's the story in your own words.

"This morning when I put the cat (Mr. Barney) out onto the screened in porch, I saw something strange in the corner where the cat always sits to watch the birds at the feeder "How did that stick get on the porch?" I thought. So ... I went closer ... NOT a stick, a snake. Picture this, I threw the cat back into the house ... went in, put on Cecil's cowboy boots (just in case the serpent attacked my ankles), and grabbed the only thing I had in the house to attack a snake with ... a large broom. When I got onto the porch, he was in the same place. He probably laughed himself silly at the great white hunter coming in his direction. I fooled him. I went out to the porch door, fixed it to stay open as I went to the tool shed. I came back with a broom in one hand and a shovel in the other. No dumb white hunter here. I did the deed and put him in a coffee can so that Cecil could see how brave I had been. Then I went into the house and took off the boots. After looking carefully under everything in the kitchen, I sat down, had a cup of coffee and pulled myself together. The great white hunter strikes again. You know how I feel about snakes. I don't care what color they are or who they are related to. A snake is a snake. This one was black and grey with a diamond pattern on his back. I still did not think he was handsome or cute."

Many thanks for a great story. Just a few questions: Has the cat recovered? Did Cecil think you were brave? Have you decided that diamonds aren't always, a girl's best friend?

My bubble burst! I had seen no snakes in our yard in at least a year. I thought the Snake Away was working. I even considered stock in the company. Any company that has a snake proof product, is my kind of company. Well, the other day I was sitting at the computer and I casually looked out the window ... bad idea. There coming straight at me was a black snake at least three feet long. I kept watching and he kept coming. When he knew he had my attention, he raised his head, and stuck out his long tongue. I could have sworn I heard him snicker as a turned and crawled toward my neighbor's yard.

Well, the snake that took off is back ... and he brought a friend. They caveated around the back yard in full view so that I could watch every slither they made. Shields got one of them but the other one got away. We were talking to the neighbor behind us and he said he had killed three. I think I told you that the house next to him had sold. The back yard had been a jungle for years ... you couldn't even see the house. Well, the new people attacked their back yard and it is beautiful, BUT, all the snakes who made their home there scattered to our yard and our neighbors' yards. This is another job for Super Snake Away. You never know when the remaining snakes will decide to launch a united attack.

In case any of you are planning a trip to Guam, don't. There was a program on TV about Guam. There are no birds and there is precious little wild life BUT there are millions of snakes ... brown tree snakes. It seems one came over on a boat during the war. They can stay pregnant for years and lay their eggs when things are most favorable. They have tried everything to eradicate them ... nothing works. They get in homes, and stores and if you are foolish enough to go out at night, they will get on you. They love to operate in the dark ... and yes they bite. So, if you have a ticket to Guam, I'd encourage you to get your money back.

I was feeling really good. I had seen no snakes and had decided to endorse Snake Away. Then, the other day I was out in the yard when my neighbor stopped to talk she had something to tell me. It seems that while we were away, she saw a very long snake climb out of our flower bed and slither down the drive way and across the street. Trying to appear calm, I said, "Was it a black snake?" She assured me it was not. I then asked, "Did you see it return to our yard?" "No," she didn't. She had better things to do than watch for a snake. I casually walked out into the street to see if I might see the last remains of a flattened snake. There was none. Perhaps he has decided to live across the street. This is not a Lassie come home situation. I guess I will get out the Snake Away and hang out the unwelcome mat.

STORIES

I have decided the world is a much safer place. I am hearing fewer and fewer snake stories, so perhaps 1) the snake population is decreasing, 2) we're closing our eyes more often, 3) we are staying inside, or 4) the snakes are hiding out, planning new strategies for terrorizing the world. Take your choice. Personally, I prefer # 1.

~

My 70th Birthday

Dear Family,

I wanted to relive my wonderful surprise 70th birthday week and share the feelings I had. First of all, "thank you." If I lived for a hundred more years and thanked you every day, it wouldn't begin to express how much I loved and appreciated what you did.

Thursday, May 6th,

Dad brought me a dozen red roses. Beautiful and they smelled so good.

It was girls' night out! Marci, Margaret and I headed out to a favorite Thai restaurant of her and Pam's. I received my first clue via Pam's great imagination. (Chad, I felt like you when you find the first clue to a treasure hunt). It read:

> *Mom, Thanks for taking time for girls' night out.*
> *Pretty soon you'll know what it's all about!*
> *Tonight's dinner will set the right pace;*
> *We'll talk and we'll laugh and we'll cheer up the place.*

…and we did. I had delightful food that I had never had before. Love that peanut sauce! The phone rang and it was Pam saying she was on her way. We ate a little more and the phone rang again. Marci said it was Marvin and asked me if I wanted to talk to him. That is an opportunity I wouldn't miss.

We started talking when all of the sudden Marvin's face was in mine. I am glad I have a strong heart. Everybody in the restaurant was laughing and enjoying the surprise. "Thank you for coming home, Marvin. Thanks for hugs and chatter and all the fun you bring with you. Thanks for you." We ate and we ate and then headed home and a second clue:

> *With the arrival of your LA son,*
> *Your birthday weekend has just begun.*
> *Tomorrow is your birthday, the 7th of May*
> *Tomorrow's surprise will help you face the day!*

Friday, May 7th,

I got up ... realized I really was 70 ... and loved it. When I was younger I never thought I would live to see the new century come in, but I did. Seventy is pretty old, I guess but I don't feel old. I believe there is a young girl who lives inside of women. The world never sees the young girl but she is there. One thing I have learned is that there is never enough time in one lifetime to do all the things you'd like to do. So, what time you have, you live it the best you can and you try to make a difference in the lives of the folks who cross your path.

Back to getting up; we had breakfast and then Marvin said it was time to go thrift-shop browsing. We like to do that. We hopped in the car but we didn't go shopping. Marvin took me to an elegant beauty shop for a facial. That was a first for me. Talk about being pampered. I was given a special gown to wear, music played some of my favorite relaxing music, and the facial began. It was incredible. My face thought it belonged to someone else. It has only known Dove soap and Oil of Olay. For a whole hour I lay there with wonderful, sweet smelling creams and steam giving my face what it had never knew even existed. Thank you for such a special birthday gift. Another clue appeared:

> *Now you're relaxed, face scrubbed and clean*
> *We hope you have been pampered like a queen*
> *We hope you will forgive us a few white lies*
> *When you get to Sonny's and find your next surprise.*

We stopped by the house so I could put on some makeup. (My face felt so good ... it still does) I didn't want to scare anyone. When we arrived at Sonny's I was surprised to see you, Joel. I thought you were working. I thought how nice that you would take the time off to come. All of you had the biggest smiles on your faces. I turned, and hiding behind a menu was Paul. I had walked right by him. We hugged and hugged. Thank you, Paul, for coming. What a fantastic surprise. Sonny's food is always good but today it was extraordinary ... family makes everything extraordinary! Another clue appeared:

> *The arrival of your Washington son is surprise number three*
> *What do you think your next surprise will be?*
> *You'll have to wait until later tonight*
> *But you'll know the answer before you turn out the light.*

Joel and Paul took off to see Bill Speakman, and the rest of us scattered until later in the evening. Amy and the boys, Marci, and Pam came by to visit. Paul and Joel returned. After a few minutes, I heard a voice behind me saying, "Hi, Mom, where's the Pizza?" It was you Mark. What a joy to have you home. I loved that hug. Another clue appeared:

Now that you know surprise number four
What do you think is still in store?
Don't plan a thing for Saturday noon
Your brood is all here, you'll know your next surprise soon.

Everyone left. We visited some more and then bedded down: Marvin in the back room, Gail and Margaret in their regular room, Mark on the couch in the living room, and Paul on the couch in the Florida room; shades of yester years.

Saturday May 8th,

Ball game day. Clayton played at 8:45 and Zach at 10. Zach, you played great. You even hit a home run. Chad was at practice at church for a program. Chad's and Zach's teams both won the championship. Those were neat trophies you won. Marvin had been off thrift shopping, returned about 11:30, and we piled in the car and headed home to dress for what I thought was lunch with the family at noon. Boy was I wrong! We headed toward the beach and stopped at Marci and Pam's church. When we opened the door, I heard "Surprise, Happy Birthday." I was in shock. I had no idea. Gail and Margaret (who we thought had left) were there, my Aunt Helen and Uncle Ben, school friends and church friends. I couldn't believe it. All of you did an unbelievable job to pull that off.

I loved the food; it was delicious.

The decoration theme was perfect. At 70, I'd like to think of myself as an adventurer. The colors green and yellow ... my favorites. You thought I might have been suspicious when we played the favorite color game around the table with the boys one night. I didn't think a thing about it. We play lots of games around the table.

Joel, the roses were magnificent. I'll never forget them. Whenever I see a yellow rose, I'll think of you. I could not believe you did such a beautiful thing for me. I enjoyed them for a whole week. Now all seventy of them are drying in a basket in the Florida room.

What lovely things you wrote for 70 Fabulous Things about Sue Moore. You are too kind. Thank you and I love you.

Having each of you children say something was especially meaningful to me. Marvin, the switch story will live on in infamy. I loved my Grandma poem. Mikey, Joshua, Chad, Zach, and Clayton, you have brought such joy to my life. Being a Grandma is wonderful. God has special plans for you boys and I am so glad I get to see you grow up. Joel, thank you for what you wrote. I'll always remember when we first discovered the pineapples on the Bringe Music store. We were so excited. The Amazing Mumford made them disappear from the story when he said, "Ala peanut butter sandwich," BUT we found them. I tried to get one for you but when they took them down years later, they threw them away. Thank you for the pineapple you gave me. You remembered. Amy, thank you for your kind words, too. You are so very special to our family. We are the ones who benefit from date night. We get to have three of our wonderful grandchildren. Thank you for putting the book together. It is a treasure. Mark, I appreciated your words, too. You will always be 'Marcus Aurelius" and 'Chef Tel', and our rock collector extraordinaire. Paul, you will always be our "angel child", our "pauley, walley doodle all the day." Thank you for the hot dog in the thermos story. Fixing lunches for you kids was a joy. Marci, thank you and Pam for all your planning and arranging. I will never forget this birthday. Thanks for what you said and how wonderfully you kept the party moving along. I will never know how you pulled it off. I still have the picture board on my desk.

The cakes were lovely. Thanks for not using seventy candles. I would not like to be the one who caused your church to burn down.

Marvin, thanks for videotaping everything...zipping around so you didn't miss anything...a bit of Hollywood in Pinellas County. Thank you, too, for making The Holiday Hound into a real book. I love it. It's my favorite of all the stories I have written. Thank you, boys, and you too, Amy, for illustrating it.

Then the last clue appeared:

Your friends and family are here to honor you!
We hope you didn't have a clue!
There's one more clue for you to get
Your brood is all here – can you "PICTURE" IT?
(Be ready by 4)

We cleaned up...packed up...and headed for home. After putting the food away to have later, we raced to Sears to have pictures made. We were quite a bunch...laughed a lot...posed...smiled and came out with great pictures. What do you expect? We're a good-looking group. The woman taking our pictures <u>did</u> survive the experience.

We returned home, relaxed and opened presents. I had not even seen the presents at the party but there was a big box full of them. So many lovely things… beautiful cards… soft warm cash for our trip…flowers… and a money tree, too. Paul, the candle in the stained glass holder that you and Jenny gave me is lovely. The lights went out on Tuesday night so we used it. The cards and the kind words were so appreciated. Many of them had poems about friendship.

We ate some of the things we had brought from the party, visited, reviewed the happenings, and called it a day.

It was an unforgettable day for me. Thank you, thank you, thank you. So many people stopped me on Sunday to say what a great time they had and what a wonderful party you all had given. I love each of you more than you will ever know.

Sunday, May 9th,

After Church, we <u>all</u> (that's what made it so special) met at the Columbia for Mother's Day lunch. Fun time…great food…and more beautiful gifts. I love the Grandma Picture frame and the red white and blue angel, plaque, and magnetic note. I look forward to reading a <u>Walk to Remember</u>. Again, the cards were especially meaningful to me. Zach, thank you for giving me your John Lynch football card. You remembered he was my favorite player. Joel and Amy, we enjoyed the visit back at your home. Thanks for taking Mark back home, Joel. I was glad you two had a chance to visit. The house seemed a little emptier. As I lay in bed that night, it all seemed like a dream, a wonderful, wonderful dream.

Monday, May 10th,

"Happy Birthday," Marvin.

Up early and off to the airport for the hardest part: saying good-bye to Marvin and Paul. We loved having you home and we missed you the minute you disappeared from sight. You are far away but always in our hearts. The house is even emptier.

I am the most fortunate Mother in the world and I thank God for each of you. Thank you for all the beautiful memories you have given me. I love you.

~

Willie

Willie opened his eyes, stretched out his little wooden arms and hopped out of bed. He tossed his scarf around his neck, put on his top hat, and smiled into the mirror. He looked great! He was ready; ready to join his family and ready to play. He took a quick look out the window to see if he was the first one up. He looked out the window to see if it was snowing. Willie let out a scream. It wasn't snowing, there was no snow on the ground; everything was green. The trees had leaves. Flowers were blooming. Something was wrong; very wrong. He hurried down the stairs. Where was the Christmas tree? Where were the candy canes? Where were the stockings? Where were the milk and cookies for Santa?

Willie looked down at himself. He wasn't melting. You see, *Willie was a small snowman*. Somehow, he'd awakened up at the wrong time of year. He was frantic. He began to look for his Christmas friends in the closet where they lived. He needed answers.

The first box he opened held the little *Christmas dish* with the small snowman. He was sound asleep. As he lifted the lid on the second box, he heard a loud, HO, HO, HO.

It was the moose whom the tall boy had brought to the house one year. Every time anyone walked by the moose, he would give out a jolly HO, HO, HO, and sing a song. Willie opened box after box but nowhere did he find his many snowmen friends. The last box Willie opened was a set of *snowmen placemats*. "You are very nice" Willie said, "but I don't remember you."

The chief placemat told him they arrived too late last year to be used. This year they hoped to be the very first box out of the Christmas closet.

"There were so many snowmen last year," Willie said. "They are my friends. Do you know where they are?"

"I think the lady who loves snowmen so much, put them in the closet over there," said the placemat.

"Thanks," said Willie, as he raced over to the closet. As he got near the door, he heard voices. Someone said, "I've checked all the boxes and Willie is not here."

"Where can he be?" said another. "It has been six months since we were packed away and all are accounted for but Willie"

Willie was very excited. "Here I am, here I am," he shouted as he opened the door. The closet was filled from top to bottom with all his snowmen friends. There was clapping and singing and laughter and even hugs. "I'm home," said Willie.

The tall snowman with the crinkled face showed Willie his empty box. Willie climbed in as the old snowman closed the top. Christmas would come again and the lady who loved them all would come, gently take them out of their boxes and decorate the house.

(For Amy for her Birthday & Mother's Day, 2013)

~

The Tiny Fairy

Once upon a time when beautiful princesses and handsome princes and fairy godmothers frolicked in the world and folks believed in the little people, a tiny fairy was born. Her hair was the color of a golden sunset and her eyes sparkled like the stars on a clear night.

"How small she is," said a tall fairy.

"Look at her wings," said another. "Surely they were spun from the night breeze as it crossed the moon."

She must have been sent for a very special mission," said the wise old fairy.

"But what can she do? She is much too small to carry a bag of fairy dust like we carry, and what is a fairy without fairy dust?"

The days and weeks passed and the months turned into years. The tiny fairy filled her days gently caring for the retired fairies and watching over the newborn ones. In the evenings, she would listen as the fairies who had been sent out into the world, returned to share their stories. "Will my turn ever come?" she asked the wise old fairy.

"Very soon, very soon," she answered.

That night the tiny fairy dreamed of all the wonderful things she might be sent to do.

The next day the Fairy Superior called the tiny fairy. "I have an assignment for you. It is not the usual kind of thing we do, but as I listened to the request, I kept thinking that perhaps this was that special mission you were sent for."

The tiny fairy was very excited. "What is it?" she asked. "What am I to do and where am I going and how long will I stay?"

"Well, you are going to the little village of Cromertown. I don't know what you will do or how long you will stay there, but you will know."

"You have no directions for me?"

"Only one; be your own special self, just like you have been here with us."

The tiny fairy spread her wings and was about to leave. "I have something for you. The elves made it for you from butterfly wings they had been saving." The tiny fairy turned, and to her delight, she saw her own bag of fairy dust. "It is magical," said a wise fairy who had talked to the elves. "No matter how much you give away, your bag will always be full as long as you need it."

And so, the tiny fairy took the magical bag of fairy dust and flew to Cromertown. She was very generous, but no matter how much she sprinkled her fairy dust, the bag was always full. Where there was sadness, she brought joy, and her laugh could be heard throughout the village. People came to talk with the tiny fairy.

"She is wonderful," they would say. "She makes us happy."

When strangers came to visit, she quietly sprinkled them with her fairy dust and they didn't feel like strangers anymore. Everyone loved the tiny fairy.

Things began to happen in Cromertown. People were friendlier. "Good morning," they would say. "Have a wonderful day." Smiles appeared on people's faces, hurts were made well and people laughed and told funny stories, and even town meetings were fun.

"Can you do this?" "Please do that." "Here is another crisis only you can handle." Years went by, and no matter what the little fairy was asked to do, she did it willingly, with love and her wonderful sense of humor. How people adored her!

And then one day, as she reached into her bag of fairy dust, she noticed it was almost empty. She wondered what had happened. Then she remembered what the Fairy Superior had said. "You will know when it is time to leave." The tiny fairy was sad and so were all the people. They remembered the good times they had shared and the difference she had made in their lives. They cried but then they smiled. "We are happy for you. You are going home and you will see your old friends. You will have another assignment and the people there will love you and you will be special to them just as you have been to us."

The tiny fairy waved goodbye and as she flew away, she sprinkled the last bit of fairy dust on the little village.

The folks of Cromertown went back to living their lives but they would never be the same again – there was fairy dust in the air.

~

The Little Hat Shop

Tucked away on a narrow winding street in the little village of Kuttlerton was a quaint little hat shop. The front was all brick, and flower boxes full of red geraniums graced each tiny window. Indeed, the windows were tiny, but oh, they were wondrous. Each was filled with delightful hats ... just the kind you would want to buy and wear. Daily, the village folks would go into the shop and come out with a fine hat on their head. The fame of the little shop grew, and people from all across the land and even beyond came to visit ... and to buy.

Now the lady who owned the shop, and was there every day except when she was away on a trip, was most interesting. She was rather tall with short hair and a twinkle in her eyes. She could talk about anything and folks loved to visit with her. She had a gentle manner and she was very, very smart.

The shop was filled with mirrors and elegant tables with clawed stools so that shoppers could sit and try on the hats and admire themselves. The lady would not say things like, "That is lovely on you," or "I think this one is more like you." Instead she would say thigs like, "Be creative," or "Be different," or "Be the best you can be." Folks like to linger and visit...but who wouldn't? The Lady always challenged them and made them feel good about themselves.

There was one mysterious thing about the shop. On the back wall were displayed a variety of hats rarely seen anywhere else. Everyone wanted one of them...BUT...there was a sign ... a very large sign that read, **Positively not for sale.** Now especially puzzling, was the fact that whenever the lady was not in the shop, the back wall was bare and the hats were gone.

Years passed and then one day, the villagers were amazed to see a sign in the front window of the Little Hat Shop. It read, "Retiring. Going out of Business. All hats will be on sale April 30th. The villagers were saddened. They would miss the lady ... she had been such a part of their lives. But there was an excitement, too. ALL hats would be on sale. The meant the wonderful hats on the back wall. Word spread quickly and on April 30th there was an incredible line of people waiting to get into the shop. At 9 o'clock sharp ... not a minute before or a minute after, the lady opened the door. In came the people and, as you would imagine, they headed to the back wall. Very quickly the wall was bare. One by one the villagers stopped to pay the lady for the hats they had selected from the back wall.

Then something totally unexpected happened.

The first villager stepped up with a Sherlock Holmes type hat. Tears came to the eyes of the shop lady and she said, "I can't sell that hat. It is the one I always wear when I go sleuthing for places for Jodi to visit when we are at a convention together." Her friends had always wondered how she could get them into those special restaurants that were off limits to most folks. Carefully she took the hat and placed it in a box under the counter.

The second villager stepped forward with a splendid varied color thinking cap with a small diamond "C" on the front. Once again, the lady's eyes filled with tears. "I can't possibly sell that hat. It is my curriculum writing hat. I've used it so many times and all my friends recognize it." Into the box it went.

Villager after villager came with their selection and time and time again, the lady said, "I can't sell that hat." Soon the box under the counter was full.

As the Villagers left the shop, they waved goodbye to the lady and thanked her for sharing her life with them. Deep down, the villagers smiled to themselves and each thought the same thought: "She'll be back."

When the last villager was gone, the lady sat down and began going through the treasured hats.

There was the mortar board that marked the day she received her PhD for the University of Texas. She smiled with satisfaction.

When she picked up the maroon and gold cap, she quickly put it on her head, and looked in the mirror. She could almost hear the cheering ... the crowd ... the marching band. Before she knew it, she began the familiar chant she knew so well, "Go Noles, Go Noles." She would always be a Seminole. The clown hat with its floppy ball on the tip brought back wonderful memories of time spent with her two grandchildren. They were the delight of her life. What fun she had finding special gifts for them when she was on her trips. "They are so smart," she thought and they have such fun on the computer when they visit.

One after another she took the hats from the box. At last there were only two hats left. One was a straw hat with red, white, and blue ribbon around the band. She had served as president of the Nurses Political Action Group and chairperson of the Political Action Education Committee. She had known what was best for nursing and she wanted anyone running for political office to know what was best for nursing, too. She had been a campaigner ... and a good one ... a great one!

Tenderly she picked up the last hat. It was her favorite, a white nurse's cap. Most of her life had been given to nursing and to the education of nursing students. She was good and students loved her. She expected great things from them and she gave so much of herself to help them become the kind of nurses she knew they could be. She had been an educator...a role model of what an educator ought to be. The Florida Nurses Association had recognized her at one of their conventions as the outstanding nursing educator in the state. How many students has passed through her classes? How many deliveries had she experienced with her students? She had long ago lost count. Ever so gently she laid the hat back in the box with all the others. "Life is good," she thought.

That evening when the shop finally closed and the lady walked out and locked the door, she carried the box of hats with her. They were all a part of her life and they always would be.

~

A Birthday Tale

Once upon a time there was a nursing lab facilitator who was moving. It was not one of those, "move at you own pace" kind of moves. It was an, "I want your house, and you have to be out by the 10th kind of moves." That might have been ok except that only gave her twenty-one days to find a place to live, decide what to keep, what to put in storage, and what to sell. It was the, "what to sell" that presented the problem. Her husband wanted to have a garage sale

And she didn't like garage sales. Oh, she liked going to them, but not having them. There was just something disenchanting about hundreds of people plowing through your belongings with as much restraint as Sherman marching through Georgia. AND then there were the hagglers, those folks who, no matter how low the price of an item, always wanted it for less. It's in their blood. She just couldn't face it.

Meanwhile, back on the ranch, really the nursing lab, her friends were planning a birthday surprise for her. They would go to Roger's for lunch-everyone loved Rogers. The problem was what to give her. It couldn't be anything for the house or yard because pretty soon she wouldn't have house or a yard. Beside that she wasn't interested in anything else to pack. They thought and thought. Finally, they had it, the perfect gift- a garage sale survival kit. Lovingly they packed it with all the things they knew she would need, and included an instruction sheet. First, they selected a box, a big rather ugly cardboard box that when empty, could be used for packing. Then they stuffed it with old newspaper to wrap her dishes in.

They had heard her say that the newspaper turned the dishes black so they added equal amounts of white tissue paper. Red or green or even blue might have been more attractive, but they had no scientific evidence they would not turn the dishes another color, too. Into the box they tucked a cup with instant coffee and Russian tea mix. Next a can of chicken soup. People say it cures everything. So she would have no dishes to wash, they tucked in a throw away cup, a paper napkin, and a plastic spoon. A box of melt away mints was added to sweeten up her day. And then, best of all a book to make her smile and feel good. Last of all they tucked in the instructions. There was a plan A and a plan B (Facilitators learned quickly that there must always be a plan A and a plan B).

Plan A

If it is a fantastic day, leave the house thirty minutes before the sale begins. Take a lounge chair, a towel, and your book and spend your day at the beach. Return thirty minutes after the sale ends, and the leftovers are packed and ready for the Salvation Army. You will still be there to count the money and tell your husband what a fantastic job he did. Counting the money will release you of any guilt you may be feeling for being away all day and your husband will love the praise. If you really want to score big points, offer to take the money to the bank on Monday.

Plan B

It is not a fantastic day. It is too cold for the beach. Retreat to your room with a thermos of hot water, you instant coffee, Russian tea, melt away mints, and of course your book. Bolt the door. Come out only to warm up the soup (if all the pots have not been sold). Make sure you come out at a time the sale is at its busiest. Then you won't be caught in the kitchen and have to share your soup. Use the throw away cup, the plastic spoon, and the paper napkin. Return to your room and stay until the sale is over. Proceed as in plan A.

Happy Birthday. We love you.

~

Balloons

I received several bouquets of balloons following surgery. I love them. They make me feel happy.

My Husband has a thing about balloons. He can't stand to see them tethered. So, after a couple of days he begins to let them go, one at a time. I can tell by the expression on his face that he is sure he has done something worthy of knighthood in the kingdom of balloons.

People are tethered much like my balloons. It isn't a ribbon or string that holds them down, it is fear, or guilt, or something that happened long ago.

Sometimes tethered people need someone like my Husband, a friend to encourage, or comfort; someone to remind them that God loves them very much and is ready to forgive the past and give them a future. The Bible tells us "You shall know the truth and the truth shall set you free."

~

Times I've Been Afraid

April 7,2014

Dear Zach,

I saw the following Facebook entry and I wanted to share a few thoughts with you. You wrote:

"Haven't I commanded you: be strong and courageous? Do not be afraid or discouraged, for the Lord your God is with you wherever you go." Joshua 1:9

"Although I'm excited to be spending the next couple of years at Taylor University, it's still scary knowing that I'm going to be so far away and in the middle of nowhere. But this verse is a great reminder not to be afraid. God is good and He has never let me down!"

~ ~ ~

You are right. God never will let you down. There will always be times that you feel scared. I was, and now I want to share a few of my scary times with you.

When I went to live with my grandparents and I had to change schools in the middle of the year. I was a sophomore.

Most of the kids were Spanish. Because my last name Garner, started with a G, I was the lone ranger in a homeroom with kids who had the last name of Garcia or Gonzalez or Fernandez. No one was allowed to speak unless it was in

82

Spanish. So I was very quiet. A friend of my Grandmother came by the house one day and asked how school was going. "Not good," I told her. She gave me some wonderful advice: "Give them time to get to know you." It didn't take long. I had 2 ½ wonderful years at Jefferson High School.

Nursing school

I was in the last month of high school. I didn't have any plans about what I would do. I was sitting in Riverside Baptist Church one Sunday morning and I had this feeling that came over me, "Be a nurse". I had never considered being a nurse. I had never been around sick people. I didn't mention this to anyone. The next morning my friend Geraldine Skipper called me and asked me if I would ride over to St. Petersburg with her, she was going to apply to the nursing program at Mound Park Hospital (Bayfront now). I went with her, filled out the papers, took a battery of tests, and met with the psychologist who graded them all. He didn't sound very promising, but two weeks later, I got the acceptance letter, and the rest is history. I loved it. It was scary at times because it was all so new. But I knew I was right where I was supposed to be.

Marrying your grandpa

I met Grandpa December 31, 1953. I was at home and went to the New Year Service at Riverside Baptist Church. Grandpa was an assistant to Pastor Abernathy. Since we had never met, Grandpa introduced himself and began telling me the latest knock-knock jokes. That was the beginning. In September of 54 he began seminary in New Orleans and I began my last year in nursing. We wrote back and forth, dated when he was home, and were married Dec. 19, 1955.

Heading off to New Orleans the night we were married in Tampa and being in Seminary 3 days later.

My first job in a hospital other than the one I graduated from. Full time job, fulltime student, and newly married.

Being a mom for the first time.

I had no one to talk to and I'd never been around babies except in the hospital and I was scared. I was a long way away from home and working and going to school, we hadn't made many friends. Mark was precious and so small. Would I be a good mom? How was I supposed to know what I was supposed to know? I was scared.

Coming back to Tampa for a year and then returning to Seminary.

Going to our first church after graduating from seminary.

Mount Pleasant Baptist Church was Grandpa's first church. Although he had preached a little before that, everything was new for both of us. It was scary getting used to being a pastor's wife. We weren't there very long before I prayed the Lord would leave us there forever. I loved it. The people were wonderful. I am sure they had some good laughs out of us "city folks" getting used to the country.

Going to our second church field.

Returning to Tampa because Grandpa's Mom and Dad were ill.

Moving to St. Petersburg.

Trying to be a good wife and mom, working fulltime and going to college one class at a time.

Going to the doctor with a problem with my neck.

Learning I had cancer

I wasn't concerned. I had a Christian friend who had had cancer and she walked with me through it. When it was all taken care of and I began those 3 month checkups, then 6 month checkups, and then yearly checkups, I found as a Christian, I was in a win-win situation. If I got a good report I got to stay around and enjoy my family. If I got a bad report, I'd just check into heaven a little sooner than I planned.

The first weeks in the Chaplaincy

It was trial and error. The people at the airport didn't know what to do with a chaplain, so it was on-the-job-training for us. It wasn't long until, if we missed a day, folks wanted to know why. It was a great twelve years. Best of all, Grandpa was doing what he had always wanted to do, be a chaplain.

Grandpa's illness

Not easy, but we were in it together. Grandpa had excellent doctors who really cared about him, and we had a wonderful family.

Life without Grandpa after he died

I miss Grandpa. Sometimes I cry. But I have had the most wonderful peace ever since he died. I don't take any credit for that; I just thank the Lord every day. Many of the women I knew who had lost their husbands told me they had seen their husbands once after they had died. I had a chat with the Lord and asked Him about it. Not long after that I woke up suddenly in the night. I was lying on my right side on the edge of the bed. I saw Grandpa's face close to mine. He didn't look old or sick; he looked like he had in college. In an instant, he was gone, but a warm feeling came over me and I knew everything was okay.

~ ~ ~

God loves us very much, and he cares about everything that happens in our lives. In his newest book, *The Question That Never Goes away – WHY?* Phillip Yancey, the Christian writer, says that we live in a fallen world, bad things happen (scary things happen) to us all.

BUT –

Christians never, never, never, go through them, alone. God is right beside us all the way.

I love you so much, Zach. I am so excited for you. God has special plans for you and you have his promise He is with you all the way.

After we moved here almost 44 years ago, your dad, who was around four years old, got very sick and was admitted to All Children's Hospital. I stayed with him. One night he woke up, crying out, "I'm scared, I'm scared, I'm scared." I sat on his bed and held him in my arms and loved him and rocked him. I could feel him relax, and before long he went back to sleep. That is like it is with God and us. We can cry out and He is right there to love us, comfort us and assure us we are His

children and He will never ever leave us alone.
      Grandma

~

Christmas

I love Christmas. I can hardly wait to put the tree up each year. Our tree is a hodge-podge of decorations. The kids made some, others are gifts from friends, some came from the dump, and a few were bought to replace those that had broken. Our tree looks like us. Christmas trees are unique and reflect the people who decorate them.

I love to stay up after the children have gone to bed and the TV is off and just look at the tree. I guess the reason I love Christmas trees so much is because so many happy memories are associated with them. I remember my grandfather, the child with polio, Seminary and Mark, the trees in Virginia, and my favorite story, *The Little Christmas Tree*.

Our lives are like Christmas trees. We have a beginning, we are anxious to grow up, we mature, and we come in all sizes and shapes. We alone choose what our decorations will be. I'd like us to think together for a few moments about some of the decorations:

The ornament of encouragement –

Sugarplums of thankfulness and patience –

Garlands of laughter (My children once said, "Mother, you laughed!" We take ourselves so seriously. If I had my life to live over, I'd take life a lot less seriously.) –

The tinsel of love. (It is important to be loved; even more important to love.) –

The star of peace –

Treasures of kindness and courtesy. (We hear the term *common courtesy*. Courtesy isn't common.) –

The light of Jesus Christ. (Just as lights give our tree sparkle, so our lives sparkle when we plug them into the power available in Jesus Christ. We sparkle and glow for Him.)

Sometimes our ornaments break or grow tattered and we replace them. Just so, in our lives. Sometimes we are not as kind and loving as we want to be. We pray for forgiveness and we have a new ornament. A tree lasts only a short time; a life lived with Jesus never ends.

~

The Warmth of Christmas

As the Christmas season approaches each year, my mind and my heart are flooded with memories of Christmases past and Pampa. Pampa was my grandfather, and if anyone could have been called "Mr. Christmas" he should have had the title. He was 6 feet 4 inches tall and quite plump and jolly, like old St. Nick himself.

Two weeks before Christmas, he and I would get out the tree lights and carefully check each one. Then we would decide what color bulbs to buy to replace the burned out ones. When we finished, we'd put everything away until the 18th. That was the night of nights. When Pampa came home from work, we'd have a quick supper and then begin our quest for the perfect Christmas tree. Our town was a good size with plenty of Christmas tree stands, and that suited Pampa just fine. We would start looking and before we were through, we would have seen every tree on every lot. Maybe the one we would finally buy was the first one we had looked at. That didn't bother Pampa. Each tree had a chance to be selected. Besides being very green and beautiful, it had to pass the test. First, I'd stand by it. It had to be at least as tall as I was. Then Pampa would hold it. It could be no taller than he. That way we were sure it would fit in the house and still have room for a star.

No matter how late it was when we returned home, we decorated the tree. I say "we" because Pampa sat in his big easy chair and supervised the whole procedure. When we finished, I could have sat and looked at that tree all night. The glass birds, the silver bells, and the beads of crystal all seemed alive in the glow of the colored lights.

On Christmas Eve, Pampa would bound in with his arms full of gifts and a bundle of wrapping paper. He would pull me aside and say, "Now don't look at this one, just wrap it." I'd know it was for me. All the others I'd wrap and fix up with special tags: With love to Sally, To My Darling, To My Best Girl and I love You Maud. They were all for my Grandmother. That's the way Pampa was, full of love and it bubbled over on all who knew him. Pampa is gone now but those memories will live on as long as I do.

~

The Little Tree

Once upon a time, there was a little tree. He was not an ordinary tree like an oak, or a pine or a Florida orange. He was a small wire tree wrapped in white, with tiny green leaves and dainty flowers entwined in his branches. He and his friends did not live in a forest; they lived on a shelf in a quaint old gift shop.

Each day. People would come into the shop and say, "Oh what lovely trees. I'll take one for an Easter tree." The little tree decided that's what he was – an Easter tree. Day after day the other trees disappeared until at last, he was all alone. People no longer passed by. He missed his friends and he was sad.

One day, the door to the little shop opened and in walked a lady. She was looking for something. She bought a few cards, paid the cashier at the desk and started to leave. Then she spied the little tree. "He is just perfect", she said as she hurried to pick him up. The little tree smiled to himself as the lady gently fashioned his tiny branches. "He's perfect ", she said again, as she handed him to the cashier. The cashier who rarely even looked at the little tree, said, "Indeed he is," as she wrapped him ever so carefully and gave him to the lady.

The lady took him to a place where there was laughing and talking. The little tree felt happy. Someone lifted him. Out of the bag. "Perfect"" she said, "just perfect." The little tree thought to himself. I'm not an Easter tree after all. I am a perfect tree…whatever that is."

The people began placing green paper on his branches and tying each piece with ribbon. He heard voices say, He's got to be very special. He is for John and Jan and Sally." As he listened, he learned that John was the pastor of their church. He and his wife Jan and their daughter Sally had bought a new home and their friends wanted to share in their happiness.

Now he knew why he had been left on the shelf so long. He had been meant for John and Jan and Sally all along. He was the one to tell them the special message their friends wanted them to hear.

As he was handed to the family, you could hear the words that were born in the hearts of their friends: "We love you, we thank God for sending you to us, and we wish you much happiness."

~

What About My Children, Lord?

In October 1970, we moved into our home in St. Petersburg. It was a mansion to us. The seven of us had lived in a one room cottage on a lake for about a year and a half. We loved it and enjoyed our time there. It is amazing what you can do with plywood and bunk beds to make a special place for everyone. Shields, my husband, worked for a private Community Relations Foundation in Bellaire Bluff. The officials had asked him to relocate to St. Petersburg. We settled in, got four of the children into school. I stayed home with our three-year-old in the day time and worked the night shift at St. Petersburg General Hospital. Shields and I had decided we didn't want to leave the children at home alone. Different shifts are not the best thing for husbands and wives but when you bring children into the world, it is your responsibility to love and care for them.

I had worked at the hospital about two years when I began having a problem with my neck. I finally decided to see a doctor. He was close to our home and had a good reputation at the hospital. When I was taken to a small examination room, the doctor came in, checked me over and sent me for an X-ray and then back to the exam room. After what seemed like a long time, he walked through the door, slapped the X-ray up on the screen for me to see, pointed at my neck and said, "You will probably have a stroke or die before you reach your car." He turned and walked out the door. I was in shock. I stopped at the desk, paid my bill and walked to my car. I made it!

As I sat in the car, the thought that kept running through my mind was "Lord, What about my children? What about my children?" When I got home I didn't say anything to Shields about what the doctor had said, and when the kids came home I didn't say anything either. I fixed dinner, we ate together at 6:00, shared our day, and laughed and talked. I never mentioned about the doctor visit or what he had said. Still the same thought came rushing through my mind: "What about my children, Lord?" I cleaned up the kitchen, checked the kids' homework, and got each one tucked away.

The next morning, I got up, fixed the kids lunches for school, gave them breakfast, and watched them as they left the house. The same thought kept running through my mind: "What about my children, Lord? What about my children?"

As I got in the car to run some errands, I turned on the radio and this song was playing. I had never heard it before.

Through It All

I've had many tears and sorrows,
I've had questions for tomorrow,
There've been times I didn't
know right from wrong:
But in every situation God gave
blessed consolation
That my trials come to only make
me strong.

Through it all, through it all,
I've learned to trust in Jesus,
I've learned to trust in God;
Through it all, through it all,

STORIES

I've learned to depend upon His
Word.

I've been to lots of places,
And I've seen a lot of faces,
There've been times I felt so all
alone;
But in my lonely hours,
Yes, those precious lonely hours,
Jesus let me know that I was His
own.

Through it all, through it all,
I've learned to trust in Jesus,
I've learned to trust in God;
Through it all, through it all,
I've learned to depend upon His
Word.

I thank God for the mountains,
And I thank Him for the valleys,
I thank Him for the storms
He brought me through;
For if I'd never had a problem
I wouldn't know that He could
solve them,
I'd never know what faith in God
could do.

Through it all, through it all,
I've learned to trust in Jesus,
I've learned to trust in God;
Through it all, through it all,
I've learned to depend upon His
Word.

Andrea Crouch

As I listened to the words. It was like God was saying to me:

"Susan, I've taken care of you all these years. I can take care of your children, too." From that moment on, I knew my children would be fine.

About three weeks later, I went to the doctor's office and picked up my X-ray. I took it to another doctor. He placed it on the screen so we could both see it. After he had spent a little time examining it, he said, "Susan, I see a little calcium, but there is no problem with the blood vessels in your neck."

I thanked him and I even gave him a hug. As I left his office, I wondered if the first doctor who had given me such a terrible report, had just been having a bad day OR if the Lord had worked a miracle in my life. I believe in miracles

Many other difficult situations have come into my life over the years. The message of this song has, without exception, reminded me of Who is always there and will see me, through it all.

~

First Christmas in My Condo

5623 80th Street North Unit 216
St. Petersburg, FL 33709
December, 2016

Dear Family and Friends,

I am spending this Christmas in my new home.
Shields and I had lived in our home on 75th Way for 46 years.
The neighborhood was changing, I couldn't keep up with the
yard work and outside maintenance, and the kids thought it
would be great if I lived someplace with more people nearby.
Marci and Pam lived at Five Towns, a lovely condominium
community, so that seemed like a good place to start looking.
We found a wonderful unit on the second floor at the end of
the Georgetown Building. It has a huge living room and
dining room, 2 large bedrooms, two full bathrooms, and a
kitchen I fell in love with. It has a window over the sink, a
first for me. The condo has windows on every side and so
much closet space.

Saying goodbye to the house was a family affair. Paul
and his son Josh came home and found a few things they
wanted to take back to Bremerton, WA. The other kids found
things of theirs they wanted to keep. It is hard to believe all
you can collect in 46 years. Marci and Pam, Joel, Amy and
Clayton, and Marvin and Phong held a huge garage sale. It
took a lot of work to get everything ready. I can never thank
the kids enough. It was to be from 7:30 to 1. Loads of
people came and we all had a fun time. About 11:30 the gang
said, "Let's tell the folks who come by now that everything is
free. They did and it left us with only 2 items to get rid of.
Great idea.

We sold our home and bought the new one and the move began. Joel rented a moving truck and Marvin invited 4 friends of his to help load the truck. Amy is the packer extraordinaire. She and Pam and I packed boxes in the days before the move.

The kids unloaded the truck, arranged the furniture, and even made the beds.

The family wanted the condo to be "country" like the house and it is. It took another day with Amy and her hammer to get everything hung up on the walls. She is an expert. She and Pam arranged everything in the drawers and cabinets in the kitchen. Fantastic! I have a wonderful family. I love them very much and I can never thank them enough for all they did.

P.S. Clayton (Liberty University 1st year) and Zach (Taylor University 3rd year) were home for Thanksgiving and they felt right at home in Grandma's "country condo".

Chad and Chelsea (who graduated from Liberty in June, married in July and moved to Texas for Seminary) were with Chelsea's family in Virginia.

Merry Christmas and a Blessed New Year.

~

Christmas 2012

Our First Christmas after Dad Died

Dear Marci, Marvin, Paul, and Joel,

I wanted to gather some items for you about your Dad; things I thought you might like to look at once in a while; things to help you know and love and respect your Dad even more than you do now (if that is possible).

There is a copy of your Dad's book, *Airport Chaplain*. Please read it as you have the time. You will discover why I say, **"Your Dad Lived His Dream."** Not a lot of people live their dream. Maybe they don't have one or perhaps things get in the way. Shields Evans Moore lived his dream: much of it in his later years. I am hoping you will see that in his book and in the other items in the black notebook.

There are items about his funeral services. I want to tell you how much I appreciate how you took charge and made the services so special. Thank you Marci and Pam and Joel and Amy for the Dad's story on the screen during the time before the service. I know that took a lot of time to go through so many pictures and put it altogether. I was there for part of it.

Thanks, to each of you who spoke at Dad's service; Marci, Joel, and Chad. So many people commented about what each of you said.

Extra -special thanks, to Chad and Zach and Clayton for help at the church and for doing the service at Bay Pines. Your Grandpa/Pepaw loved you very much.

Marvin, thank you for sharing your memories of Dad. The lady from the office, who took us to where the service was held, said she had never before heard such wonderful laughter at Bay Pines.

Paul, thank you for making that trip from Bremerton twice: once for Mark; then again for Dad. Dad loved the time he had with you on your first trip.

I loved your Dad very much. I still do. I miss him but I know one day I will see him again. I can never thank God enough for that last morning: I dressed Dad and got him into his wheelchair. I reached around the wheelchair, gave him a squeeze, kissed him on top of the head and said, "I love you, Sweetie."

I love each of you very much.

Mom

~

My 80ᵗʰ Birthday

This has been an incredible birthday; a total surprise. I can never thank each of you enough. I loved every minute, even when I had no idea what the minute would hold. Best of all, was having time with all of you and watching you interact with each other. I wish everyone in the whole world could have a family like ours. Planning all this and keeping it a secret must have been a challenge. Believe me, I didn't know a thing. My only instructions were to keep Thursday night through Sunday night open, and be packed and ready to go Friday afternoon.

This is my version of the most wonderful birthday I ever had.

Wednesday night I came home from church and found Chad in front of the house by his car. I thought he had come to visit. We went inside and Amy, Zach, and Clayton were there. I was told," Don't go out in the Florida Room." (You can see I am getting short, to the point instructions) It wasn't long before Marvin and Phong showed up, and then Marci and Pam. We were laughing and talking, when a loud voice yelled, "Get out here quick." We all tore out there to find a birthday cake with 100 lighted candles; 20 for Chad, 80 for me = 100. Chad had come up with that number. With a big blow from Chad and me we got all hundred out on the first try. It was amazing the cake did not burn up. Have you ever seen a cake with 100 holes in? Well you would have if you had been here. It was delicious. Some of us had ice cream. I opened lovely birthday cards. Cards are real treasures to me. I have years of them from the children and grandchildren. There was school the next day so the gang headed out. Did I mention how pretty the table looked with a birthday tablecloth, pink and blue ribbons hanging over the table and a happy face birthday balloon on my chair.

Thursday was a pretty quiet day. That evening, Amy and the boys showed up. Then Marvin and Phong arrived. A little later the bell rang and I opened the door to let Marci and Pam in, and there were Paul and Josh. I couldn't believe it. I just hung on to both of them with a bear hug and I didn't want to let them go. We visited for a long time, then everyone left and we headed to bed. Paul and Josh had had a long flight from Washington State.

Friday, we slept in. In the afternoon, the gang arrived in 2 cars. We girls decided we would go in one car and the guys in the other. Joel was out of town. Just before leaving the house, I was told we were headed down near Sanibel Island. Sanibel is one of my favorite places, lots of good memories. We arrived at the Marriott Hotel just before Sanibel. We pulled into the parking lot. As I got out another car was waiting to pull in next to us. I waved to the man in the car; the kind of wave that says, "Sorry to keep you waiting."

As I looked at him, I thought, "I know the man." Sure enough, it was Cecil with his wife Ann, our cousins. I was expecting them at my home next week. I stood there in shock as they parked. Hugs exchanged and we all went in to register. Our suites were wonderful and so big: 2 bedrooms a living room, 2 baths and a well-equipped kitchen. We rested awhile. Later we got frozen pizzas from Publix, some snacks, and something to drink. We baked them in our rooms, took them down to the Lobby, to a table big enough to hold all of us and enjoyed every bite. We talked and played games until around 10 before heading to our rooms. Amy drove to the airport to pick up Joel who was returning from meetings out of state. I know he was glad to see you.

Saturday started with a delicious breakfast at the hotel and then we were off to Sanibel where Marvin and Phong were staying. Joel and Amy and the boys headed for the beach along with Marvin and Phong and Marci. It was real breezy. Getting the kayaks out in the water took a lot of energy. Joel and Amy took a walk on the beach with Chad. Ann and I took it all in from the screen porch and from a long walkway. We were not the sun people. Joel and Amy and Marci and Pam had picked up an assortment of sandwiches at Publix so we all had lunch and celebrated Marvin's Birthday. He sat on the floor opening presents, reading from 2 books he received and keeping us all laughing. Some of us rested and others headed back outside until time to leave.

When we got back to the hotel, I was told to be downstairs and ready to go at 5:30 – another example of short, with authority instructions.

We all left and drove and drove and drove. I had no idea where we were headed. We finally turned in at a place that looked like a storage building and a jail. We got out of the car and heard the whistle of a train. It was then I saw, we were at the station for the Mystery Train. What a shock when I realized where we were. I had wanted to take that train for years. You have a wonderful meal and solve a mystery. What fun that was. I got to sit with Clayton. We had a great time listening for clues and deciding whodunit. I loved it; so did Clayton. Then it was back to the hotel. We needed a good night's sleep.

Sunday started with another great breakfast at the hotel. While at the table, we shared Mother's Day. Thank you for the many cards. Amy, I loved the photo of your family and me and the way you had it displayed on the word *mom*. You do so many special things. I can't thank you enough. I have it sitting on the hutch, so I can enjoy it. Ann and Cecil and Paul and Josh and I drove back to Sanibel and met Marvin and Phong for a last look at the lighthouse, a walk around the end of the Island, and a seat on the pier to enjoy the view. We headed home with a stop at Wendy's (Josh's choice). Marvin and Phong, thanks for the cookout at your home later that evening and a look at the Amazing Race. Phong your food was delicious. I love eating in your backyard and sitting around the fire. When I'm out in your backyard I feel like I am in some wonderful faraway place and I just want to take it all in.

Who would ever have believed so many treasures could be tucked into one birthday and Mother's Day. Who would have thought being 80 could be so much fun.

Thank you, thank you, thank you. Time truly is a gift and you were all so generous with your time. (And I am sure with your finances, too) I am grateful. I love each of you very much.

Post script

Monday, Marci took Paul to the walk-in clinic. The doctor gave him a shot and some medicine and we took him and Josh to the airport in the afternoon.

Cecil and Ann had 2 items on their "to do list". One was to eat a Cuban sandwich for lunch and the other was to have dinner at Carrabba's. We accomplished them both.

Tuesday, we had Mondays left overs (from you know where) and brought in ribs for dinner. Thanks to each of you for coming by to visit one last time with Cecil and Ann and Paul and Josh before they left.

I called and checked on Paul Tuesday afternoon. He sounded really good and said he was feeling great. He gave the doctor's injection credit for that.

Wednesday about 10 a.m. Cecil and Ann left for TN. Suddenly the house was very quiet.

Thursday. Thanks for the invitation to share in Amy's birthday dinner at Season 52.

It is a lovely place, great food, and I loved all the conversation around the table.

~

STORIES

FAMILY MEMORIES

FAMILY MEMORIES

Meet My Family

Since you have seen the names of my family in the first section of this book and since you will see them even more in this section, I'd like to introduce them.

Shields is my husband. We were married in 1955. He died in 2012 after a long illness. I met him when he was the assistant to Reverend Abernathy at Riverside Baptist church in Tampa. We met on New Year's Eve in 1953. He spent much of the evening telling me knock, knock jokes. All through his life he shared jokes with everyone. Even when he began writing weekly Chap Notes with a Bible verse and stories, there was always a joke. When he was in ICU, everyone who came to visit him shared a joke that he had told them. The nurses said they had never heard so much laughter and they loved it.

Mark was our oldest son. He was born in 1956 while we were in seminary. He died one month before my husband. He had ALS. Mark served in the army. He later married Kay. She had three children from a former marriage so Mark became their Papa. Mark loved landscaping. He could make any yard beautiful.

Marci is our only daughter and she was born in 1958 in Tampa. We lived on a lake. After a trip to see the mermaids, Marci decided she wanted to be a mermaid. Her Dad setup a bicycle on the dock and attached a long hose. As long as someone peddled the bicycle, Marci could carry the hose, swim under water, and receive all the air she needed. She was indeed a mermaid. Her Dad became her hero forever. Marci is a writer at heart.

When quite young she wrote and produced a neighborhood newspaper called *Justice*. She and Pam have spent 21 years consulting throughout the U.S. with nonprofits in financial crisis. Pam is now the CFO for an international education organization. Marci is a writer, speaker and founder of Show Up with Love, an organization committed to teaching love as the cornerstone of compassion and healthy communication in our homes, workplaces and communities. As she likes to say, "Change in the world begins with change in our hearts."

Marvin was born in 1961 in Virginia. At birth his hips were turned in. He wore special shoes and at night a bar between the shoes to keep his hips in line. He has always been the family comedian. Those who meet Marvin say, everyone should have a Marvin in their life. He was a magician, he later moved to Hollywood where he worked with the Simpsons. Following that, he traveled on the road with Miss Saigon as the massage therapist for the dancers. Sometime later when Joel and Amy had their three boys, he decided he didn't want his nephews to grow up without an Uncle Marvin and he moved back home. He and Phong have a Marine Upholstery business.

Paul was born in 1962 in Virginia. Marci had hoped to have a sister, not a third brother. I heard her praying by his crib, "Please, God, change him into a girl." Paul could sell anything. When the other kids had things to sell for projects at school, they would ask Paul to do it for them and he did. He joined the Navy and retired after 20 years. In his last years in the Navy, he took locksmith classes. Now he is a locksmith at a Navy Base in Washington state. While in the Navy, he met and married Jenny. Jenny had a son named Mikey from a former marriage. Paul adopted Mikey and 4 years later he and Jenny had Josh.

Joel was born in 1967 in Tampa. He is in medical sales. If one word could be used to describe Joel, it would be integrity. When he says he will do something, he does it. When he says he will be somewhere, he is there. Joel is married to Amy. She wanted to be a stay at home Mom and Joel wanted a stay at home wife and Mom. They are a match made in Heaven. They have 3 sons: Chad, Zach, and Clayton. It has been our joy to have these boys most Saturday nights until Chad was 15 years old, so Joel and Amy could have a date night. After that, Joel and Amy thought Chad needed that responsibility. They are fine young men. They love God, they love family and they give best to everything they do.

I love my family very much

Enjoy your walk through this family section.

~

Shields

Eighty Fascinating Things about Shields (Husband, Dad, Grandpa)

1. Radio operator in WWII.

2. Taught the kids to "land ski" by pulling them around on a cardboard box attached to the Volkswagen bus (at the lake house)

3. Taught his children to be entrepreneurial – anything honest to earn a dime

4. He knows how to make the most of space – he packed 5 kids and 2 grownups in a Honda Civic – and later in life, shocked Pam by fitting a 4-drawer file cabinet in the back seat of another Civic

5. Loves words and has a seriously great vocabulary!

6. He could make anything. He's the original MacGyver.

7. He electrified the bird feeder so the squirrels couldn't get to the feed

8. He made us a barrel swing. I guess he had a thing about barrels because later he found enough olive barrels to build a floating dock on the lake.

9. He is a great story teller and his sermons were always full of colorful stories

10. He sings beautifully and was the very first song leader for the church in Charles City

11. He kept us in line in the front row pews by correcting us every once in a while, from the pulpit.

12. He gave us all our love for sweets. As kids, we mostly used all our extra earned money to buy candy and sodas – except as the boys got older, they used theirs to buy model car kits.

13. He made a hot air balloon with a dry cleaner's bag, straws and a couple of candles. We watched it go up and out of sight.

14. He encouraged us to start Justice – our neighborhood newspaper and helped us figure out how to make copies to sell.

15. He was a farmer in Virginia and had some pretty good crops.

16. He let us walk to Foxes Corner, at least one hundred miles away from the lake house, by ourselves.

17. He scared us half to death whenever we camped, whether we were in the middle of the woods or camping in the back yard, by coming out and making noises like a bear.

18. He took us to the fair and encouraged us to ride the wildest rides – just to see whether we would throw up or not.

19. He made "FOUND" toys – the giant wooden cable spools that we rolled around the lake house and used as tables or just stacked them up like giant Legos.

20. He caught giant frogs with his bare hands.
He plowed a straight (we'll, almost straight) row with the help of a borrowed mule.

21. He preached through the whole book of Genesis.

22. He is and always will be a chocaholic.

23. He has been writing and editing Chapnotes for 19 years

24. He has been a volunteer Chaplain for the Tampa Fire Department, Palms of Pasadena Hospital and Tampa International Airport.

25. He used to deliver day old bread to earn a little extra money.

26. He gave me the best gifts I ever received: Mark, Marci, Marvin, Paul, and Joel.

27. He always has a story or joke to share. Always gives the boys new jokes to laugh at.

28. He started the Chaplaincy at Tampa International Airport

29. He loves cigars. Great cigar smoking buddy.

30. He never worries about combing his hair.

31. He is a good husband.

32. He knows how to slide down the pole at the fire station.

33. He drove a limo.

34. He is a deacon.

35. He used to hunt deer with a bow and arrow. Don't look for a trophy. Those big sad eyes of the deer got to him every time and the arrow never flew.

36. He was a bee keeper.

37. He is an avid computer user.

38. He makes the world's greatest fudge: chocolate and peanut butter.

39. Dad's fudge skills now include the daily crossword puzzle!

40. He has tremendous patience with tedious tasks of his choosing – sewing fishing nets.

41. Dad can make boards into boats.

42. Dad can save a vacation using only a penny and foil (the time we rented a trailer and we arrived at the campground after dark only to discover there were no fuses in the camper...dad saved the day).

43. Dad helped produce some really great kids.

44. Dad has become an amazingly accepting father.

45. Dad helped start the chaplains program at TIA. Which has helped more people than we will ever know.

46. Dad can weave a cast net from fishing line and then go out and catch dinner.

47. Dad is a great teacher of the cast net throwing arts.

48. 80 years of giving great hugs.

49. Grew great strawberries.

50. Dad drove a bus for the mentally challenged – and when he wasn't driving the bus, he parked it directly under the cherry tree so we could climb on top and pick all the cherries our bellies could hold.

51. Dad taught me my multiplication tables and I really appreciated how he taught me to multiply by nine. Great trick!

52. Dad gave us all a love of reading. He read the comics to us every single Sunday.

53. Dad helped us appreciate the bigger world by asking us to pray for the missionaries doing work throughout the world. When we were kids, each night at dinner, we would pray for missionaries and put red push pins in the map of the world where those people served.

54. Great at inventing challenging "toys" for the squirrels to work up their appetites before feasting on the bird food.

55. Great host to any *stranger.*

56. Hey, Dad learned from Nancy Reagan, "Just say no."

57. Brought us home the best presents even though they were free. Refrigerator boxes that became forts and olive barrels that became a raft.

58. Taught us all to be resourceful – to have a full life whether we have a little or a lot, to try things, to be open to new experiences, to travel whether it is fancy or frugal.

59. Taught us to find the way to say I can instead of I can't. Just think, three of your five children – no, four including Paul and his real estate venture, either work for themselves or create their living entirely upon what they produce, create, find or sell. All of us are lifelong learners thanks to you.

60. Gave us a taste of adventure and experiences in nature early on – Sharp Top, Flat Top, camping in North Carolina, sliding down slick rocks in freezing cold mountain streams, going on hikes and swimming with alligators. Your thinking must have

gone something like this – *"hey, if my kids can swim with the alligators and survive, they can face anything life throws at them."*

61. Amazing ability to keep the car on the road while simultaneously swatting evil doers in the back seat. Must be that driving with your leg thing he taught us early on.

62. Taught us boys the life skills we would so surely need like using a coke bottle as a make shift urinal or a water pik to keep toe nails looking their sparkling best.

63. Built the infamous mermaid contraption that all the lake house neighbors envied.

64. He was a teacher in the public school system.

65. There were a lot of drive-in movie visits in Lynchburg, but I don't remember a one.

66. Vacations with rock collecting themes -   Georgia gold, amethyst and starolite.

67. When I graduated basic training, dad came up and stayed overnight. We went to the Jersey coast.

68. Dad's suggestion that I should consider a summer away from home on a tobacco farm.

69. Master coat hanger mechanic.

70. The original "Abithinathy" story teller.

71. Great travel companion to Arizona and a true adventurer.

72. A Wonderful grandfather to his 5 grandsons.

73. Great Father-in-law.

74. Awesome cheerleader at the boys' sporting events.

75. Great haircut test subject--when Joel cut Dad's hair when Joel was little.

76. Wonderful babysitter for the boys.

77. A wonderful part of the welcoming committee when each of the boys were born and Great arms to swing the boys when babies.

78. Always ready to listen to the boys' stories and jokes.

79. Endures the thanksgiving lunch at Keswick every year just so he can eat with the boys and is a welcome visitor every year at Keswick's Grandparents' Day

80. He always found a way to get me the weird presents I wanted for Christmas, like Danny O'Day and the unicycle.

And some to grow on from Mark and Kay:

81. I once asked why don't they have "Kids Day," you know like "Father's Day" and "Mother's Day." Dad replied, "Every day is Kids Day."

82. Our fishing trip on an all-day deep-sea fishing boat. All the guy relatives went.

83. Building swings and a raft at the lake.

84. The drive-in movies.

85. The vacations built around rock collecting.

86. Dad came up for my Basic Training Graduation and us going to the Jersey Coast.

87. My first car, he showed me how and what "gapping" a spark plug was.

88. He rented a sail boat for a family sailing trip.

89. Cigars on the porch.

90. His specialty cooking fudge and taffy.

91. Finally, I find so much of what I do, how I fix or rig something, how I think, my sense of humor, and my values, all have their roots in my Father.

92. Stepping up and being a Grandfather to Shawna, Kym and Gary; attending their activities like baseball games, band programs, etc.

93. Front porch swing talks.

94. The most special of all is when he married Mark and I, making our day complete.

95. I am blessed to have a Father-in-law like you.

~

What I Have Learned at Age 79 Nearly 80

At age 79, I have learned that God loves me to love others; that some of the biggest wealth in this world are the gifts of laughter coupled with faith; and that God really has a purpose behind the need of sharing ourselves with Him and with others!

....Shields Moore

My Thought During Christmas 2000

These walls have known much laughter
These walls have seen some fears
These walls have known a godly faith
These walls have seen our tears.

Our home holds such memories
Of things that used to be
Of childish games and happy times
And dreams that set us free.

So now we have our golden years
No punching the time clock anymore
We watch the struggles of our young
And pray them more victories than pain.

... Shields E. Moore

~

Fifty Wonderful Things about Mark

1. Our firstborn.
2. The oldest sibling.
3. A super marksman.
4. A landscape artist extraordinaire
5. A hard worker.
6. Can grow anything.
7. Served in the military.
8. The Chef Tell of the Moore clan.
9. Husband
10. Father.
11. Grandfather.
12. A Miami Dolphins' fan.
13. There is nothing he can't do in the yard.
14. Once held an alligator in one hand (we have a picture to prove it)
15. Likes to work on old cars.
16. Good fisherman.
17. An excellent driver.
18. He has a great laugh.
19. Was a fabulous tree one Halloween.
20. He's a wonderful camper.
21. Runs at top speed when being chased by wasps.
22. Loves pecan pie.
23. Heard the most "AbdatheNathy" stories.
24. Fun game show host. (We remember that Christmas)
25. He is a survivor.
26. A fearless swimmer.
27. Fun to be with.
28. Very creative.
29. Knows how to economize.
30. Makes a good campfire.

31. Stays in great shape.
32. Can climb a cocoanut tree.
33. Loves to read.
34. Can chase armadillos.
35. Super tree climber (even with a cast on his leg)
36. Knows how to avoid getting shocked by an electric fence.
37. He will break an arm and a leg for you.
38. Can out run dogs.
39. Expert computer game man.
40. Super little league baseball player.
41. Can leap high when stepping on a stick he thinks is a snake.
42. Talented merman.
43. Enjoyed buying candy at Mrs. Binns' store.
44. Had a pet possum.
45. He is adventurous.
46. He listens well.
47. Helped raise Myrtle the pig.
48. Later ate Myrtle the pig and said, "Boy, this Myrtle is good."
49. He is patient
50. There is only one Marcus Aralias and we love him very much.

Happy 50th Birthday and Many, Many More!

~

Building Bonds

By Mark Moore

To Dad on his Seventieth birthday September 10, 1999

Building outdoor playthings for my kids was usually spur of the moment requests: "Dad, can you…?" or "Dad we want to…," and I was off.

Being creative is easy. My mind would think of the possibilities. "We can do this," or "I can do that," I would say. Then reality came around. Resources were limited. Whatever we had on hand or could find was used. Sometimes a trip to the hardware store was necessary and my basic collection of tools would have to be hunted down. Often a hammer or saw would be found under a tree silently rusting away from the boy's last project and I would scold them. In that moment, something familiar came back to me. My Father's voice telling me to put things back where they belong.

I don't remember all the things my Father built, but each child remembers his favorite. There was an olive barrel swing with real strong rope my sister and I would swing on. When another brother or two came along, there was another tree swing and a tree house. After church on Sunday, we would climb up in the treehouse and I would be the preacher.

When we moved to Florida, we lived on a lake and my Father built the four of us a raft to swim out to and jump off. It was built with four wooden barrels, two by fours and plywood, and lasted a long time.

It was about this time, I was eleven or twelve, my tool "use and lose" lessons started.

Looking back on my Father's creativity and resourcefulness, I see where I got mine from. He was a much better wood worker than I am and the time he mounted an air compressor on a stationary bicycle so we could breathe air from garden hoses under water, no one has forgotten.

My projects have never been so grand: a ramp for bicycles, a basketball backboard. They served their purpose. They may be remembered or forgotten But I remember. The great visions of craftsmanship have bowed their collective heads to simple function, a child's wish, and a Father realizing his limits.

Thank goodness for love.

Thank you, Mark. Dad and I love your writing. What wonderful memories you bring back.

~

Messages from Mark on His Computer

(Mark died 3/22/2012)

This starts with the last message I received

Note: Our Son Mark had ALS. He could not speak and had no control of his muscles. He used to say before he lost his voice, that he had a great, wonderful brain in a dying body. The only way he could type messages was for someone to place his hand on the keyboard so he could drag one finger to the letters he wanted to print. That is why there are many misspelled words. PLEASE, DO NOT CORRECT THE SPELLING. These messages are a real treasure to me.

3/21/2012 Mark's last message.Ihad the new threapist come by yesterday afternoon. Amber is really good. OF course i can relate to dad and short furniture. I can't get my leg muscles to coperate either.how ever Amber is going to work on that. no special plans here but we have a thhhirty percent chance of rain. tAKE CARE IN THE YARD. LOVE MARK

3/19/12 I didn't feel good this morning and then the bath lady showed the same time the new pt showed up. How is dad feeling today? I wish we were closer too. love, Mark

3/16/12 have said it before but i love you both and miss seeing you. Dad, smoke a cigar for me. Mom enjoy your new floridaroom for me. love mark

3/14/12 know what you mean about sliding in bed. In my hospital bed too. I HAD TO RAISE THE SPEED BUMP UNDER MY BUT. ok get a good night sleep. lov e mark

3//9/2012 its that of day when you say what are we having for breakfast? Me, anything liquid and donn't forget the coffee.Ihave detached myself from the worlds problems. That maybe why i don't watch t v. Anytime there is bad news i say to myself i haven't got much longer and then it is someone elses worry. I hope you have a great day. Smoke a cigar for me dad. love,Mark

3/7/12 Allan just left. I haven't seen him since he stayed at your place. he was here about an hour. hope your day is well love mark

3/6/12 i just wanted to let you know i am still here. love mark

3/5/12 i just got my internet connection back. Windstream lost its broad band signal during the storm and i just now got it back. The storm was a slow mover and it spent so much time in the panhandle by the time it got to us there was nothing left but rain. love mark

3/5/12 I know you are watching american idol. So i wanted to wish you all a good nights sleep. Love, Mark

2/25/12I got home yesterday about seven. Kay told me about dads situation last night when we got settled. I am happy to be home but i can't walk very much any more. I got Marcis note. All is well around here. They claim lake wind advisory here but i want to who has a lake. A kite flying advisory would be more suitable. Anyway, have a good day, love mark. p s i had now internet at all this time

2/4//12 What a strange coincidence, me too. I found a website that has 5000 patients with als. It is called patients like me. of course i got my first message from a sephen hawking character who has als for 20 years and thaths not bulbar. i doubt very seriously there are many people who are in there i don't plan to be long as soon as my left hand stops working i am over it. I am glad you found some garage sales the weekend of the first of the month is the best time around here. Take it easy, love mark

2/5/12 It is a shame that Superbowl is on a sunday and more people watch it than attend church but then again the bible says broad is the gate that leads to destruction .On the other hand the Bible says all things are lawful but not profitable. Am i taking these out of context or what. Just thought i would ask. Love,Mark

2/03/12 Well, what does the world have planned for you today? Me i am being good. I am sitting in my trusty wheelchair and all have left for appts. So i shall not get up the risk of falling is too great. Anyway, i plan to do the usual. Kay went with Kym to the Shands neurosurgeon to see whats up with that and Lisa just left for a doc with one of the girls. So it is just Maggie and me. She barks i don't. Love,Mark

12/31/11 Sitting at the computer for the final time this year. Does the church have a watch night service? Come monday a cold front comes thru and we will be in the twenties.

I am not a fan of cold weather All is quiet here. Happy new year to you, dad, family and friends. Love, Mark

12/27/11 I am doing as well as expected. I sent a happy birthday note to Joel i believe he is 53. But i know my days are numbered. I would hope this winter because it is the winer of my life. Spring is out of the question since everything would have to be done for me since my arms and legs are going. I wnt my independence, productivity. If that is taken then so am i. I would wish for a miricle but this was meant to be. love, Mark

12/22/11Wish i could walk with you. It is pretty mellow round here. Kay went with Ashley to let her pick some outfits that she will like at JCPENNYS. She and lisa have spent the last few nights wrapping gifts. Iam no help there. I may get my wish and be alive for christmas and at home. Well, that is it here. Love, Mark

12/19/11 Thinnkiing of you two today and what you started 56 years ago. Hope you sharewondful today. love you mom and dad,Mark

12/16/11 I have not written till now because early wenesday morning i was in bed and went to use the urinal laying down and discovered that my feeding tube had come out. Good thing the hole closes on its own or i would have discovered a new meaning for an empty stomach. Well Kay drove me to the hospital around 2am and went to the emergency room which is a good time to go they weren't busy but in no hurry. While i was there i asked for a chest x-ray to see if i needed a "bronk" while i was there. They said some fluid had built up on the outside of my lung and they admitted me to icu as a boarder and sent Kay home. Later she told me she had started to fall asleep at the wheel twice. But in the mean time the docs made tha rounds and i said i needed a bronk and then go homme. They did that at 10am and i left the hospital in an ambulance and got home at 200pm Kay had to run into town with frank and billie to get them a spare tire cause they were leaving friday. i fell asleep for 2 hours and woke up feeling short of breath and took my oxygen count it was in the low 80s. so i tried to get oxygen know that nap had built up co2. anyway it was a rough night but i slept with oxygen. and waited for kay to wake up and say good bye to billie and frank before taking me to the computer. So Kay has had little sleep in 4 days on account of my health. But i am feeling better now. love, mark

12/26/11 Twas the day after christmas and all thru the house toys lay everywhere including the mouse house. The wrapping paper so neat before was crammed in large garbage bags by the back door. YOU GET THE PICTURE. Kay hadn't slept in close to 3 days. Thankfully i was able to unhook myself from the vent and get to my chair without incident because she got after 4pm. So life does go on. I am glad you got your kitchen back in order. that refridge we got five years ago and replaced with a new one still works and we bought it for a hundred dollars in Citra and after i bought it i saw the back said made in 1989. and i thought it wouldn't last long. that was a heck of a clog. Maybe if you pour diet coke down the drain it will keep it clear.i am contemplating coming down soon. love mark

12/25/11 Well, i didn't go shopping because let me count the ways but those who did deserve a sentence. Not only did they buy to much but now i can't get thru the house. So, i here by sentence myself to a life of celabacy. Not that is hard to do in my condition but because i have a sense of humor about how people relieve stress and guilt, when the only thing these kids need is more positive attention. That is my christmas report and i am sticking to it. Love, Mark

12/23/11 I am not sure if i spelled it but next year in april i signed the papers on this house 18 years ago. This year was the first we have carolers come by. Of course they were from church and they said they were coming by but it was delightful. Kay and Lisa are still wrapping gifts. Me, i am doing what i do best, next to nothing. Thats about it here. Hope this message finds you cozy and in a festive spirit. Love, Mark

12/ 16 /11 Me too. I went with them to get christmas tree. I sat in the van and watched the people come and go with pine trees. So, i am back on puter while they get things ready for christmas. I am not in the christmas spirit and i don't want anything for christmas than to be alive. Love, Mark

12/2/11 I sometimes would like to eat again but if i want real flavor i can put a little in my mouth and my taste buds still work and spit it out after the cheap thrill. I am the only one i know that can eat all the chocolate i want and not gain an ounce. Oh well. it has been a good day so far. But reality raises its head once in a while. Kay is stressed and noone can do her job since gary likes to hang out in jail. Oh well, we don't have things disappearing like we used too when Chris and Gary used to steal and pawn things to support their expensive drug habits.

We lost a gun, the chop saw frank had is gone, etc love, Mark

11/30/11 Sorry for not writing sooner, like you, the day ran away. It was good. EVERY DAY I CAN STILL WALK AND USE MY LEFT ARM IS GOOD. Anyway, Kay got the dogs some flea and tick repelant that works for 30 days.We have had way too many tick show up on buster lately. He is a mellow dog but big and not too bright except when it comes to opening doors. He can do that with his teeth. But he has a hearing problem, he doesn't listen to commands.iT IS LIKE TALKING TO A KID. hope you sleep well too. Love Mark

11/26/11 well, by now i am sure all your running around has ceased. The van hasn't been converted yet. When i went to Tampa, they put everything on hold so it is red tape stopping us not undeceidedness. It has been cool but our next cold front comes late tomorrow. We will be in the 40 come monday or tuesday. We haven't done any decorating yet. We are still recovering from thanksgiving.I think they will get a real tree this year. Anyway i haven't done much today. OR any day lately. Just plucking away at the only thing that i can do any more and that won,t be long either. When my arms can't do any more and my legs give out it is time to move on. Love, Mark

11/23/11 yep. nothing but grandkids going all over the place. me, i am getting ready for bed. Happy Thanksgiving to our family and friends which are the extended family. Love, Mark

11/22/11 Well, i made it home after 48 hours in ICU.

Just needed a broncostimy. I am not sure about the spelling but is a way of life lung. I like watching the camera crawl around my lung. Anyway, Frank picked me up Kay is sick so i am noy moving around too much with out walker or wheelchair. My right leg gave out the other day. I couldn't up in my bedroom so i crawled across the floor banged on the closed door and allysa found me and went next door where was visiting Billie and Frank. Frank was able to get me up and i layed in bed awhile got back on computer and later got a fever of 102.6 , took the ambulance to VA in gainsville and got bronked the next day and sent me home with more antibiotics. A nd, that as Paul Harvy is the rest of the story. Love, Mark

11/11/11 I am sorry to hear about Jennys surgery. Kay and i can both relate to not walking. I have no plans for today. I would like to get to walmart or best buy and get some speakers for the computer and another wireless mouse. I find it amusing that restaurants will feed vets for free tomorrow and i can't eat. :(Oh well, have a great day. Love, Mark

11/2/11 The dynavox came on time put my wheelchair bar on, and showed kay how to put it on and take it off. He isnstalled the eyemax but in the end he removed it because he has been around alto of ALS patients and he said i wasn't ready for it , i am too mobile. Besides, with eyemax on it won't sit on a table. So a good was had by all and my dynavox is up and running again. wAITING TO HEAR HOW YOUR DAY WAS. lOVE, mARK

10/22/11 Well we didn't make it to the store yesterday because the nurse came late. So this afternoon we went to walmart, the dump and get gas. It has been a while since i went into town besides going to visit hospitals, so it was nice except that i have to wait for people, avoid getting hit on a scooter and scooters aren't made for people with als. my back starting hurting while riding around and i have to be careful with my neck when people drive. The little things like that puts everything into a whole new perspective. Anyway, enjoy the boys and we are on top of things here. Love, Mark

10/18/11 THEY NEVER SAID WHAT TYPE OF ALS ME I BEIEVE IN WHAT THEY SAY ABOUT BUBAR. BUT EVERYBODY IS DIFFERENT. I HAVEN'T FELT TE PRESN C ED HE WAS TA LK ABUT AND I DON'T GET THE GOOD AN D FAITHFUL SERVENT AWARD.B UT I HAVE SAVED IT. LOVE MARK ON LY A SPRINKLE ALL THE HYPE AN D IT SEPLIT NORH A ND SOUTGH

10/2/11 Hello mom, just getting started with the day.Living in the moment is easier when i don,t know when my time is up but knowing all signs are there. Mainly my muscle loss below my rib cage. At 120 puonds i would dare anyone to fatten me up. hope your day goes well. love mark

8/30/11 Well, the big day is finally here. Who would have thunk after all we have been through in our life together we would be celebrating our 20th Wedding Anniversary. Happy Anniversary, Kay. I love you. This will be my last anniversary and last birthday. My body lost too much muscle in all the wrong places. I will be suprised if they don't keep my in the hospitalagain next month nd give me a trach. I have been holding off bt my lung capacity has dimished alot. So, i take one day at a time. I hope you and have a great day. Love Mark

6/21/11 I am glad to hearVBS went. well. I will try to get some things done around here. Kay saw Char and Barry yesterday. Its the first i have seen them since before my diagnosis. I can't talk or eat anything anymore. I am thinking of getting pallitive care. I get my medicine when people wake up after noon and the breathing machine they sent has been used once. My lungs are my weakest link. Anyway, hope your day goes well. Love,Mark

6/7/11 I have had two cups of coffee with cheese cake minus the crust. Any hot liquid will melt the stuff. Same with chocolate ice cream. I am in the experimental stages but anything other than vanilla ensure is the cats pajamas. I put a little in my mouth for the taste, wash out my mouth and the rest goes down the g tube. Curtain call! Love Mark

5/21/11 I have been doing that kind of stuff for most of my life. If i couldn't affrd it, i rigged it. I am going to have a busy monday. I hope it doesn't intefere with your visit. I love you and dad. Thanks for putting up with my crap.

5/ 6/11 Your mothers day gift should arrive on monday. Love Mark

4/20/11 you are taking care of the magnolia all right. You will find many trees lose their leaves in order to pro create. Many trees hae no foliage till blooming season is over. On the other hand the contaminated ground water could have an effect. Give it your best like you give me and it will show. Love Mark

4/11/11 I was wondering why yahoo didn't show mail today. Then i found i hadn't signed in. Oops my bad. Speaking of snakes, we killed two of them recently. **uster is taking a liking to the canal. I am afraid he will get bitten but there is nothing gonna change. So, kay sera sera. The "Mark Moore memorial shed arrived this morning.** *would live in it but we have alot of things to store. If i really want an adventure i will sleep in it one night. My legs are getting weaker. If i were to fall who knows what will happen. But i am in Gods hands I just wanted get it over with and not this slow wasting away. I am sure there is a eason. I love you and dad. Ma*

3/21/11

Thanks mom. I had planned to write this morning but my doctors visit was this afternoon, so i waited to let you know it was good. They said i looked good and my blood and oxygen levels were fine. Vitamine b 12 is up and i need a potasium boost. So, I survived another day and make my doctor laugh with what is on my computer. That's a first. Good luck with the yard. I don't have much energy, so it's wing it. I love you and dad.

3/15/11 good morning mom and dad. The trip back went without a hitch. It was great being surrounded by family. I almost felt like there was nothing wrong or normal. Trips to anyplace but the hospital make me feel better. Rental goes back by noon/ Weather is great . I might get something done. I hope you and have a great week.Love Mark

2/21/11 Well, i had grown tired of working hard and not having enough to do extra let alone the bare necessities and

God knew my heart. I wasn't hip on the idea of having to retire and work to make it either. The bottom line is not being angry with anyone for this. I accepted it as payent for alot of wasted life. So i look at a rare disease for a common man as a plus. I only don't want to prolong it so i am a vegetable.Besides,one day they might find that the army wasn't responsible. So now i get paid to stay home and waste away with all sorts of things that make my life easier. I hope that clears that up. I do have some moments of saddness but the way the world is going i am not going to miss much.That's about it for now.Thanks for your letter. LoveMark p.s. the kitchen will out last me

1/18/11 We spent the better part of the day at Gainsville VA. It is warmer today. Nothing new to report. My breathing is good until lay down. That's why i have a sleep machine and an oxygen machine. Otherwise it's one day at a time. Kay is still suffering from a URI. Today wore her voice thin, so it will be a few days of typing.Of course mine ain't getting better. I my have a call from the new dynovox rep so they can put my talking machine on the chair and maybe get the open phone hooked up. Keep me posted on Aunt Caryolin. Love,Mark

1/15/11 Yes,everyone had good time.I was suprised at dads patience.I don't know today will bring. with the weather in the 30s and highs in the 50s there was little to do outside.Just going to thedump or local store was a way toavoid cabin fever.I suppose Kay will want to get out for awhile and shop for Kayrons bithday present. Goodluck garage saleing.love Ark

3/19/12I didn't feel good this morning and then the bath lady showed the same time the new pt showedup. How is dad feeling today?   I wish we were closer too. love, Mark

12/31/10 Sitting at the computer for the final time this year. Does the church have a watch night service? Come monday a cold front comes thru and we will be in the twenties. I am not a fan of cold weather All is quiet here. Happy new year to you, dad, family and friends. Love, Mark

~

Poems Written by Mark Moore, Age 16

A Friend for Me

Somewhere in this world of woe
I'll find a friend at last
Who'll shed a light upon my trail
No shadow he will cast.
We'll work and play together
We'll live so peacefully.
Somewhere in this world of woe
I'll find a friend for me.

~~~~~

Love, Perfect Love

There are some things money can't by
Like my love for you till the day I die.
I live for you, you love me
Our happiness is plain to see.
Our love is perfect, it has no fear
I long for you to always be near.
My words are nothing compared to my love
With its fondest dreams of you my dove.
There are some things that money can't buy
Like my perfect love for you till I die.

~~~~~

A Christ like concern for all people
I pray for each day and each night.
I long for Christ's love to fill my soul
So I can lead his sheep to the light.
I thank God for answering prayer
And giving me a Christ like love,

So I can use my talents
To glorify God above.

~~~~~~

Life
What is life?
Why are we here?
Does life end in death?
No one Knows.
I guess that's life.

~~~~~~

I'm 16 and you are 11
But still I'm thinking of you.
Your sky blue eyes, your golden hair
What can I do but love you?
I searched my life to find an angel
That'd turn my life to heaven,
But when I found my dream come true,
I cried because you were eleven.

~~~~~~

My Lost Dream

Her long golden hair flowed down her beautifully
        tanned back like a river.
Her sky blue eyes seemed to pierce into my mind,
        seeking out my thoughts and emotions.
I longed to kiss her ruby red lips and tell her how much I
love her,
        but my thoughts are in vain
            She loves another.

~~~~~~

Christmas

Christmas time is wonderful for those who know it well.
Besides the lights and Christmas trees a story it does tell.
A story of a baby who born on Christmas Day
Shed the light upon the world so they might know the way.
He taught us how to love and live abundantly
So when we leave this world we'll live eternally.
This is why we celebrate nativity
Because He loved us very much, He died to set us free.

~~~~~~~~

Wow! July 4, 1998. Fireworks at 8:30 Saturday morning?
No, just the explosion of thoughts racing through my head
as I sit by the lake in our yard. A novel could be written,
but where to start? Past? Present? Future? A mind trained
in guilt and worry can easily blend them all into a picture of
now.

I'm in my country home, barking dogs, singing
birds, and chirping bugs are the dominate sounds besides
silence. In the distance train whistles mark the passing of
scheduled time and autos faintly verify another work day in
progress.

A turtle head appears in the lake. The mirrored
reflection on the water is broken. A snake bird sitting on a
stump, drying its wings, cries out. Beyond this lies a vast
sea of lily pads and their countless white blossoms.

Perhaps this is the best time I have of living in the
moment. Soon my wife will arise and get ready for work. I
am a morning person and this is "be quiet time." I think of
all that needs to be done. There is so much work I want to
do but I must quell my desire to do anything that would
disturb her sleep.

Coming back to the country after 30 years sure has
changed from the simple carefree times I knew as a child.

My ideas about what it means to be "countryfied" are changing all the time. What a novel idea.

Mark Moore, age 41.

~

Remembering Marci

To Marci from Mom
April 17, 2004

Thanks for the chance to remember and to write these memories. There's no special order. As I went back in time I wrote them down as I remembered them

1. You never swam at Weeki Wachee but you will always be my favorite mermaid. Tube in your mouth, someone frantically pedaling the bicycle, you were in a water world all your own. I always wondered what you were thinking.

2. You on your unicycle. Dad on one side and me on the other soon gave way for birth of a possible circus star. We watched in amazement.

3. You and Chatty Cathy. "My name is Chatty Cathy and I love you very much."

4. You kneeling by Paul's crib and praying, "Please God, change him into a girl."

5. The Christmas Eve I had to sleep with your present under my head to keep you from opening it.

6. Your face the Christmas you opened your gift from us. It was a little key. Your comment, "Oh isn't this cute." Until we suggested it fit something, you thought that little key was your gift. You were surprised when it fit the secretary; something you had said you wanted someday.

7. The way you would walk around at the lake with Joel on your hip. You were quite the big sister.

8. When you called from college and said you had nothing to eat. $10 was all we had to our name and we sent it to you.

9. The trip to the canyons where you became the poop and paw expert. According to Marci: If the poop was too big and didn't look too old, turn around. If the paw print looked like a mountain lion, make a lot of noise and walk fast. If you spied a bear, stop and don't look him in the eye.

10. Another Marci lesson learned in the canyons: If you look deep in a canyon and spy what looks like ants but turns out to be people, do not hike down without food and water (lots of water) and remember, going down is easier and quicker; getting back up is another story. One also gains a new appreciation for rocks…big ones…the ones you can collapse on at each switch-back along the trail.

11. Marci Model on the runway. Your hair was long then.

12. Your turquoise bedroom.

13. When you were a baby, you played the baby Jesus and lay quietly in the manger at Riverside Baptist Church.

14. Thinking about Christmas, our baby Jesus was rarely in His manger. He was in your pocket.

15. All seven of us piled into the VW Bug with our groceries inside and a Christmas tree tied to the top.

16. Camping in the mountains and hiking the trails. Remember when we climbed Sharp Top Mountain. We climbed on our hands and knees the last 45 minutes. We learned later it was a haven for snakes…we didn't even see one. We didn't think it would take so long to climb up and down but it did. Dad had to call and cancel the evening service because we couldn't get back in time (and he was the preacher).

17. Mrs. Binn's store and the penny candies.

18. Hiking in the creek and having to run from a wasp nest.

19. Trips to the library in Richmond to get enough books for a month at a time. Remember *Mostly Fredrick Sometimes Sam* and *Bactus and Carius?*

20. The youth choir with Cecilia.

21. The Great Valentine. He found you wherever you were.

22. The years at the lake house. You lived in your swimsuit the whole summer unless we went somewhere.

23. The old swimming hole in Rustburg, Virginia.

24. Grandma Moore and the aluminum Christmas tree.

25. The first time you drove the car.

26. You went to TN to major in journalism, were told to switch to teaching, got to your interning and decided there was no way you were going to teach, came home, got tested, were told you would be great in accounting and business. You said you were terrible in math, they said that was ok because this accounting math was different. You graduated from USF and LOOK AT YOU NOW!

27. Remember when you bought your first house. We thought you were amazing.

28. Climbing out the window onto the roof of our house in Charles City.

29. Eating cherries from our trees and grapes from the vines in Charles City. At cherry and grape season, I never wondered where you were.

30. Crying in the restaurant when you learned the Great Valentine had retired.

31. The fun you have being an Aunt.

32. Daddy carrying you up the stairs to our garage apartment when we brought you home as a newborn from the hospital.

33. Picking blackberries in Charles City. Dad would mow a path around a big clump and we would pick.

34. Picking blueberries and blackberries on our canyon adventure.

35. The little three-legged beagle. There is a great picture of you and Mark sitting on the back steps at the parsonage in Charles City holding him.

36. Making Brunswick stew in the big black pot and all the relatives coming to help and to eat.

37. The first day of hunting season when you couldn't go outside because buckshot would hit in our yard from hunters who weren't too good at shooting.

38. Myrtle the pig. She was little when we got her. You all knew she was being raised to eat. When the time came, the man appeared, shot the pig and left. Dad and I dragged Myrtle to the bathtub. A couple showed up and fixed the pig. We cooked down the pig fat to a liquid. We set it on the back porch to cool. You stepped in it and we could only thank God it had cooled enough it didn't burn you. The first time I cooked and served the meat, you and Mark said, "This Myrtle sure is good."

39. Remember the night the lid blew off the coal stove and covered all of us with thick, black soot. When we heard the explosion, we ran in to check on you and Mark. There you were sitting up in bed, looking like a couple of little black children.

40. Remember the swing set in the dining room in the winter when it was too cold to be outside.

41. Christmas shopping at the dime store in Williamsburg. We would take you one at a time to shop for each other. You even wrapped the presents yourself.

42. Cutting our Christmas trees. In the woods they looked so small, but in the house, they touched the ceiling. Remember making paper decorations for the tree and having our church family in for cookies.

43. Remember making hundreds of cookies and freezing them for the party.

44. How about the gingerbread house Aunt Judy would send each year and we would put it together and decorate it.

45. Remember Rustburg and snow and sledding. It took longer to get everyone dressed for the trip outside than the time we spent outside. Remember roasting hotdogs and marshmallows when we came in.

46. It was fun to have a basement.

47. How about those "deadly, deadly" hunts we went on?

48. Going to the movies on Sat. night with Dad and picking me up when I got off work.

49. Working at Suncoast Mental Health.

50. Seeing you and Aunt Sylvia together.

51. Singing the Twelve Days of Christmas around the player piano, Marci style, "Hello Mable."

52. You are making a difference in people's lives. You are helping them to make the second most important decision they will ever make. You and Pam make a good team. I see the encouragements on your walls and I notice the way you deal with each other. You are good role models for the business you are in.

These are only a few of the things I remember. I want to keep remembering, but for now, Happy Birthday and many, many, more.

~

Happy New Year, Marci & Pam

May it be a very special year for each of you.

This has been a very special Christmas for me, and I thank you for all you have done to make it so memorable.

Thank you for the lovely bathroom cabinet and basin. It came as such a surprise. I am really enjoying it.

Thanks for cookie baking night at the house. Thanks for all you two did to get ready for it. That day would have been Dad's and my 60th wedding anniversary. That's why I think the cookie party was held that day/night. I think you kids did not want me to be alone. I have a very special family. I love Dad and I miss him very much. It is hard to lose the love of your life. The front door opens many times, but it is never Dad. Thank you for your thoughtfulness.

I have enjoyed having you and Pam at the house. It has been fun watching you look for a condo. The one you now own is beautiful. It will be even more fun, watching you design it to be you.

I had a great time on the cruise. Thanks for helping make the trip possible. My very favorite time was sitting around the table with the whole gang. It was so precious to me to watch and listen as you interacted with one another. Your faces, and your laughter, and talking. Maybe it is a "mom thing", but I loved it.

Had some quiet time sitting out on the balcony and watching the waves and listening to the sound. That was nice.

Loved being at Ponchos. The fun at the table, the food, and the music was wonderful. When I realized I'd been there before, thank you for reminding when it was.

Thanks for taking me back to the ship with you for a nap before dinner. Naps are good.

Thank you for a very Merry Christmas and memories to cherish the rest of my life.

I love you,
Mom

~

Mom's Memories of Life with Marvin

My mind and my heart are filled with memories of you. This bag holds a few reminders of some of those memories. There is no special order and by no means is this all. **Keep in mind this is the way I remember.** Now, Marvin, you may remember it differently but that brings up a point. When you remember something from the past, I always wonder if your memory is really that good or if you just had an incredible imagination.

Charles City

1. Pair of shoes labeled right and left: When you were born your legs were twisted at the hip. You wore reversed shoes when you were awake. At night you wore a brace with shoes that kept your hips turned out. You kept getting the brace caught in the rails of the crib, so as a baby you slept in a bunk bed (bottom bunk of course). As you reached the crawling stage, did this bar slow you down? Not on your life. One night we heard you crying. When we went to check on you, you weren't in bed. You had crawled down the steps and were sitting in the middle of the living room floor wondering where the rest of us were. When you began walking, we would take you to Richmond. So many people would come up and tell me, "Don't you know your child's shoes are on the wrong foot?"

2. Jar of honey: Dad had a bee hive. One day I found you sitting right in front of the beehive watching the bees flying in and out. You did not get one bite. I must confess, I did not race over to rescue you. I calmly called, "Come on, Sweetie, it's time to eat," (or some such thing). And you came.

Rustburg

3. The Coke Bottle: Not an aluminum can, a really truly glass coke bottle. Remember when we were driving to Tampa one time and all of you needed to go to the restroom. (It was lucky Marci had to use it too, so we stopped. Normally, Dad told the guys to use THE coke bottle. (That was definitely not a girl thing.) When everyone (or so we thought) was back in the car. We took off. I don't remember who looked back, but there you were running toward the car, waving your arms and yelling for us to stop. Since you are here, you know we stopped.

Florida

4. Favorite Treats: Peanuts. Maple nut goodies, wedding cookies, Krystal Burgers, Krispy Kreme donuts. To this day, if you are in Tampa, near Krystal Burger, you'll bring home a sack to share. Dad cut a path around the blackberry patch. You were hooked on blackberries once you discovered the ripe ones.

5. Magic Wand: You are the magician extraordinaire. In the 10th grade, you were in the talent show at Bogie. We all went to see you. As other kids got up and performed, the audience booed. I couldn't believe people would do that. When you got up to do your magic act, I thought and might even have said, "If they boo Marvin, I'll kill them." The audience loved you and your magic and not a boo was heard. You did a magic act in elementary school. That was good, too. I loved all your magic but my favorite was your close-up magic.

6. Telephone Book: In high school, you would make a bee line for the bathroom the minute you got home. (It wasn't safe to use the restrooms at school). You would take a quick peek around for something to read; seeing nothing, you would grab the phonebook. As you disappeared into the bathroom, you would say, "There are lots of funny names to read." Laughter could be heard in the bathroom.

7. Dogs in your life: Waddles/Duchess/Oats/Rickey.

8. Your tennis shoes thrown up on the elective lines that took everybody's electricity right at supper time.

9. You and your Tuba. Parades and concerts

10. Kermit the Frog. After your accident, you didn't want to go anywhere in your wheelchair. It was the first Kermit Movie that persuaded you to go somewhere. Over the years when you went to the beach and someone asked about the scar on your leg, you said, "Shark attack."

CA Days
10. Calls from CA when you or your friends were ill; Mom/Nurse in Residence 3000 miles away.

11. Coming home to visit. The first thing you did when you got home was to run through the whole house and make sure nothing had changed. Then you would take everything out of your big wooden trunk, relive a few of your own special memories, put it all back, and then head out to visit friends. Later when Oats came with you, he would do the same thing, except he would settle down in his bed.

You have given us many memories. There is only one Marvin. Everyone should have a Marvin in their life. We love you so very much; you are our Marvelous Marvin.

~

Dear Marvin

Dear Marvin,

I had the most wonderful time when you took me to see Wicked. I won't ever forget it. You are so much fun, so loving, so caring and you have such a gentle, tender, heart. A day with you is a treasure. I saw this cup and thought of you. I ordered it but it hasn't arrived in time for your birthday. I am so sorry. As soon as it arrives, we're going to breakfast and celebrate again.

I love you very much. We both love you more than you will ever know.

Happy Birthday, Marvelous Marvin

~

I Hope So

I was supposed to be writing my resume' but instead I am drawn into a conversation my father is having with his mother in the room next to me. You see, my grandmother is very old and the medication she takes often confuses her so that she cannot recognize her own children. She often asks for Henry my grandfather who died last year.

"Is this your house?" my grandmother asks.

"Yes it is." starts my father's monologue. "I've lived here twenty years and I am buying it. Before that I lived in your house by the lake and before that Richmond, Virginia." As my father speaks, I see all these places, too, but from much younger eyes and I can tell from my grandmother's comments that all this information is painfully new to her. "I was in the Baptist Seminary...." my father continues, reciting his entire formal education.

"Where do you live?" my grandmother asks again.

"I live here and I've lived here for twenty years", replies my father patiently. My grandmother mumbles something." You have nothing to worry about. We are taking care of you. Whatever you want, we will get it for you. We get your medicine and if you need to go to the doctor, we will take you there.

You don't need to worry about anything", my father said, sounding like Father Knows Best.

I can't help wondering what it will be like when my parents get very old and forgetful. Will I be able to love my parents even when they don't know I am their child? God, I hope so. I love them so much. .... *Marvin Henry Moore*

~

155

Dear Marvin and Phong

Happy New Year
May it be a very special year for you.

As I look back over 2015, one of my happiest memories is going to garage/estate sales with you and Kinky Boots on many Saturdays. You two are so much fun. Marvin, you have a real eye for value and I am always amazed at what you find. I also notice you are always looking for something Phong would like. It is very special of you to do that. Thanks, Phong, for letting me steal him away for a while.

Thanks for cookie-baking night at the house. That day would have been Dad's and my 60th wedding anniversary. That's why I think the cookie party was held that day/night. I think you kids did not want me to be alone. I have a very special family. I love Dad and I miss him very much. It is hard to lose the love of your life. The front door opens many times, but it is never him. Thank you for your thoughtfulness.

I had a great time on the cruise. My very favorite time was sitting around the table with the whole gang. It was so precious to me to watch and listen as you interacted with one another: your faces, your laughter, your talking with each other. Maybe it is a "mom thing," but I loved it.

Loved being at Ponchos. The fun at the table, the food, and the music was wonderful.

Thanks, too, for your help in making the trip possible.

Thanks for helping me get around the ship when it was rocking and rolling.

Thanks for a very Merry Christmas and memories to cherish the rest of my life.

I love you, Mom.

~

Paul Moore's Writings April 1997

If I Could Be Anything or Anyone

Many years ago, my mother told me, "Paul, you can be anything you want to be." Only five at the time, it hit me; I wanted to be a bird. I was serious. The thought of flying high up in the sky, only needing food and shelter, but most of all, to be free to go wherever I wanted to land. My mother smiled and explained what she really meant, that I could be anything within reason and that birds are not people.

What I want most out of life is not fame or fortune, but wisdom and knowledge. To me, that is something you cannot put a price on. You see I have never really been good in school; one of those slow learners; but that would change. First, I would go back to school and get my degree in engineering and English. It's because I like to study machines, how they work, and the history behind them. This is why I would study engineering. Why English? That is simple, I wish to learn more about the language. With two degrees under my belt, I would teach others at a vocational school. You see, there is something else I would do. I would teach in my spare time and read all the great books ever written. When I think about what would be harder, learning to fly like a bird or going back to school, hitting the books is a lot safer.

Movies

Long day at work or school? Wanting to get away from it all? Go see a movie and escape! Here you can be anything, go anywhere, or just get lost.

Welcome to the world of motion pictures!

I, myself, like the older pictures as well as some of the newer ones. Looking back over the years, one can see how much the movies have changed.

Good points: movies in color, stereo sound, special effects, and video cassette recorders.

Bad points: more sex, more violence, and more obscene language.

How much sex, violence, and obscene language is too much? Every year we find ourselves lowering the standards on what is right and wrong. It's up to you, for we are the ones that decide what shows are good or bad. Just think, where do we go from here? Or worse, where will we be in ten years?

Life after the Navy

It's going to be different for sure. After ten years in and having everything there for you, now it's up to me. With less than six months left, I'm behind the eight ball already. Trying to get caught up on bills or just to pay them off is enough to cause gray hairs. On top of that, trying to find a job that will pay me the same, if not more, than what I am being paid here. At times like these, you have to have faith. Good I am single and don't have a wife to drag into this. What would I like to do? Well I am hoping for a locksmith position with the Veteran's Hospital in Seminole, Florida, just outside of St. Petersburg. That is my home of record and my parents still live down there. With luck, I hope to be working within a few weeks of getting out.

Here Today for a Better Tomorrow

I'm not here to talk about my life story or what I've done or where I've been. No, instead, I would like to tell you where I'm going.

My life has been on hold for a long time, filled with many hopes and dreams. Looking back now, I only see yesterday, as all the tomorrows that have come and gone. For this, I have only myself to blame. There is so much I want to do, yet, so little time. I'm forever giving people advice, yet never really "practicing what I preached". As I write this paper, it's as if I'm hearing myself for the first time. You see, that is why I am here in this class today, for a better tomorrow. Next time I turn around, I want to see my dreams and hard work of yesterday become the realities of today.

Blinded

The ad read, 1968 Impala convertible only $625. Now that is something I'd have to see for myself. It was a beautiful sunny day when I pulled in front of the house. It was no mistake, that was the place and there it was. Yes, the soon to be, first convertible of mine. She was long with a black top and a metallic blue paint job. It was love at first sight. All I could think about was the thought of me behind the wheel of that car. The guy came out and showed me the car. It had a 327, small block engine with a four-barrel carburetor and power top. By this time, I was sold but there was still the test drive to take. (Most people would drive the car themselves), Not me; for he drove the whole two minutes. He drove the car nice and slow. As for me, I was in another world.

It wasn't until after I bought the car that things started going wrong. First, was the oil. There was none! Six plus quarts later, she was full. You might say it sucked more oil than gas. Every time I would push the pedal, this black cloud of smoke would appear from the back and engulf any car behind me. It was the James Bond car. Later, a hydraulic hose broke, causing the power top to become manual. Sure, it had its share of problems but I loved it just the same. If I had it to do all over again, I would.

No Snakes!

I've had a number of pets over the years, like cats, dogs, gerbils, and rabbits, but never a snake. You see, my mother is deathly afraid of snakes. She never met a snake she didn't hate. Just to see one on TV or in a book would set her off! A friend showed her a three-dimensional picture once. The kind you have to stare at for some time until it jumps out at you. Well, it did just that. The picture was of a rattlesnake ready to strike. She has all kinds of stories to tell about snakes. Ask her about snake repellent or the famous snake mirror. What is a snake mirror, you ask? First, you take the old tinsel off the Christmas tree. Next, sprinkle it out in the yard where snakes might go. The whole purpose is that the snake sees itself and is scared away. To her the only good snake is a dead snake. That is why I never had a snake as a pet.

Birthday Suit

(My most embarrassing moment)

It would have to be the time back at the lake house when I was six or seven. You see, school was out and summer was at hand. Mom would hand out swim trunks that we would live in for the next three months. Life on the lake in the summer was great for a kid my age. This means I did not have to take a real bath and could run free until the street lights came on. At this point I would head inside and get ready for bed. Not saying I'd go there. We only had a radio and time was spent with the family and not the boob tube as we know it today.

Like all nights it came and went and as the sun arose,

so did I. Not to miss any of the coming day, I got up and went to see the lake. Walking down the path only ten yards from the water, it was then it hit me. I forgot to put on my swimsuit. I was outside in my birthday suit! So, I ran back to the house before anyone could see me. It was truly embarrassing and something that I thought I'd never forget. Thanks for reminding me.

Lasting Impressions

Who, has meant the most in my life?
Who, is near and dear to my heart?
Who, fed and clothed me?
Who, loved and cared for me?
Who, taught me right from wrong?
Who, protected me from harm?
Who, gave me the courage to carry on?
Who, are the ones I care about?
Who?
My Mom and Dad
That's who.

Pork Roast, Sauerkraut and Mashed Potatoes

My favorite food would have to be pork roast, sauerkraut and mashed potatoes. It's been a long time since I had such a dish. Not that I didn't want it, just that I have been away from the family that used to make it. The dish itself brings back a lot of good memories along with some bad. You see my x-wife's mother and grandmother were the cooks and great ones at that. The dish was usually served on the first of every year. It was said to bring good luck. I just thought it tasted great and could never get enough.

The sauerkraut was first rinsed, so not to be too tart

and then it joined the pork roast. As it cooked, the aroma filled the house along with the anticipation of the up -coming meal. Her Dad loved the dish as much, as if not more, than I did. He taught me to enjoy it, and most important, how to fix my plate.

First, depending on your appetite, one or two big scoops of mashed potatoes. Then pile on the sauerkraut, not forgetting the broth that it was cooked in, and top it off with black pepper. If you have any room left on you plate you go for the roast. If not, don't fret, it won't be long until there is. Of course, there are biscuits and honey and desserts to follow. You could say I miss my favorite meal. Kind of makes my mouth water just typing about it. It has been five years sense the last time I had such a dish, but I feel it won't be long before I enjoy it again.

I Take Pride in One's Safe

Although I have had a number of proud moments, the ones that stand out the most are every time I open a safe all by myself. No, I'm not a thief. I'm a locksmith for the Navy and my job is to get into safes while doing as little damage as possible. I enjoy my job and take great pride in each and every undertaking. I'm unable to put into words, the feeling I get when I hear the click or the handle turns and the safe doors open. The first thing I do is thank God for giving me the knowledge and skill to perform this job. Then I turn the safe and its contents over to the owner as they show their gratitude. Just knowing that I perform my job to the best of my ability and that the customer is happy; it's not just a job. It's an adventure.

My Vacation!

They say, home is where the heart is. Well, at least for the past ten years mine has been in St. Petersburg, Florida. You see, I'm in the Navy and for the past ten years I have been stationed everywhere else but Florida. So, when I go on leave, it's off to St. Petersburg I go. To me it's the simple things in life that make the difference; like spending time with my family, helping my mom and dad around the house or doing things with my brothers and sister. Many nights I think of this at work. As for me, it's quality time spent with my family back home.

My Hometown

Welcome to my hometown, St. Petersburg, Florida, home of the newly wed and nearly dead; if you are into CB radios, it's referred to as wrinkle city. You might gather from these nicknames that a big part of the population is retired.

The only history I know about the city is that it was named after St. Petersburg, Russia. (Chamber of Commerce). While you are down town, check out the pier. It's a newer building with an unusual design. It's shaped like an upside-down pyramid and stands six stories high. Inside you will find plenty of gift shops, food stands, and my favorite, the three-story aquarium. Now it's off to the top, 4 or 5 stories up and we're on the roof. For just 25 cents you can see downtown, from the boats in the water to the people in the park. If it's food you are looking for, the Columbia Restaurant is just below us. I highly recommend the Cuban sandwich, black bean soup and chicken with Spanish rice.

After a good lunch, it's time to head for the beach. Whether you like fishing, swimming, sunbathing or boating, it is all here. From putt-putt golf to gift shopping, it is truly a tourist's paradise.

Just in case you are thinking of moving here, the average price home is $75,000 for three bedrooms, one and a half bath. The employment here is good for jobs of all kinds.

St. Petersburg is also a good location. We don't see the real big storms that the other parts of Florida get. Thank you for taking the time to read about my hometown. I hope you enjoyed the tour as much as I enjoyed giving it.

Thank you, Paul, for sharing yourself in your writings. We love you very much.

Thank you for allowing me to share your writings in my book, *Memories from the Attic of the Heart.*

~

Happy Father's Day to Paul

June 12, 2016

Dear Paul,

Happy Father's Day to you.

I love you very much and I am so proud of you. You are a good man and everyone who knows you, loves you. You reach out to so many people with friendship and encouragement. You are a good listener and an amazing helper. Whenever your name is mentioned, people smile.

You are a good Dad for Mikey and Josh, and you have been an excellent example for both of them. You are also a good husband. You take fantastic care of your family.

You are the greatest s'more-maker of all time. Evenings sitting around the fire in your backyard and eating s'mores is a joy. On my list of my 10 favorite things to do, that is my number-one favorite. I don't get to do it very often, but I love it when I do. Thanks for such a fun memory.

Thanks for your phone calls. I love to hear your voice.

I thank God for you and for how very special you are.

Enjoy your Father's Day.

I love you.

~

A Christmas Letter from Jenny, Paul,

Mikey (16) & Josh (3rd Grade)

I wanted to write and let everyone know how we are doing. As some of you may know, we had to put my Dad in an Alzheimer's facility in December. It has been a difficult time for our family but we have felt your prayers and appreciate the support. I wasn't on top of sending Christmas gifts this year but our hearts and prayers are with all of you. My Mom is learning to live on her own for now and we are taking each day as it comes.

Anyway, the kids are doing great. This year, Mikey went on 2 mission trips; one to Mexico and the other to Suriname, South America. Both trips provided experiences that he will never forget. We are sending out DVD's to the families that supported him financially and more if we can. We were only given six. Mikey turned 16 and got his driver's license this year…WOW.

He also had his first EP (5 songs) produced and made and is currently for sale on ITunes. Mikey leads worship for Youth Group and Church twice a month.

Josh is in 3rd grade at Peace Lutheran and doing wonderful in school. He has parts in all the plays and is an A student. He loves Legos and in September started taking Tae Kwon Do lessons. He has taken 2 tests so far and has his green/yellow belt. It is amazing how much they have to remember. He loves playing Star Wars video games and playing with our Corgi's Mookey and Samie.

Paul is still at EJB, a government contractor for the Navy, as a locksmith. He retired from the Navy Reserves this past February with 20 years of service. He helps out with all the church functions and lends a hand whenever needed. He definitely has a servant's heart. Paul was our chauffer during the last blast of snow and loved playing in the snow as much as the kids.

Paul and I are still working fulltime while we also work on building our real estate investing business. We currently own 3 investment properties and rehabbed and flipped one this year, and are working on doubling that in 2009. It is something we enjoy working on together and believe it will give us more options in the future.

I had surgery again this year in May and had 3 more stints put in. The good news is that those stints improved my blood flow tremendously and I'm walking again.

Well you may have received more information than you wanted in this letter, but I never seem to get a chance to let friends and family in our lives know what's going on and how much we appreciate all of you. It has been a great and challenging year. We pray and hope that all you have a terrific holiday season and a blessed new year!!!

Love,

Paul, Jenny, Mikey and Josh Moore

~

Fifty Wonderful Things about Joel

1 You have integrity.
2 You are a loving Husband.
3 You are a "hands on" Dad.
4 You are an excellent provider.
5 You are a fantastic Son.
6 You are kind.
7 You are generous.
8 You work really hard.
9 You are a fine Christian man.
10 You are fun to be with.
11 You are Mr. computer man.
12 You are a sharp dresser and you like nice cars.
13 You are handy around the house.
14 You are a Brother to be proud of.
15 You give your best whatever you do.
16 You introduced the family to "sticky feet".
17 You are the "million- dollar boy".
18 You remember (example: The pineapple)
19 You bring us incredible joy.
20 You have dreams and you dare to follow them
21 You want the best for others.
22 You are real
23 You are the captain of you own "ship."
24 You make a difference in the lives of others.
25 You can (and do) play practical jokes.
26 You are a survivor. Three older Brothers and you're still alive to tell about it.
27 You have a tender heart.
28 You expect the best of other people, even when they disappoint you.
29 You have a great laugh.
30 You love birthday parties.
31 You are original piñata man.

32 You know the best places to eat. (Example: the hotel in Phoenix).

33 You are brave. You took your parents on a family vacation.

34 You are a fun, loving, and wise family oriented Brother.

35 You are willing to go the extra mile.

36 You are a motivated, goal oriented, successful Husband and Father.

37 You are a Super sports fan.

38 You are always ready with a funny story to get us laughing.

39 You are full of surprises. I will never forget my 70 yellow roses.

40 You are fully committed to whatever you do.

41 He is fearless. He will lead his family through Alligator infested water in the Everglades and managed to get them out safely.

42 He is the guy you want by your side in a crisis. He's level headed.

43 He's the guy you want to have fun with. He's up for pretty much anything legal and before 11PM in the evening.

44 He is a beach baby. He loves sand between his toes, collecting shells, and eating at his favorite restaurant in Sanibel.

45 He started the annual siblings cruise several years ago. In my book, he gets a medal for that alone. Each time we discover how all of us are more alike than we are different. Together we have gotten through illnesses, losses, and life challenges because we purposely get together once a year-away from the rest of the world for friendship, bonding and fellowship

46 He put God first, his family second – and is a real friend to many.

47 He picked Amy, the perfect wife, who stood by him and saw the possibilities in a young man ready to make his mark on the world.

48 He excels at leadership and coaching people to perform their best.

49 He along with Amy, raised three tremendous boys.

50 He put up with going to Miller's Ale House almost every Monday night when he was in town, just so he could eat my favorite dish while going through cancer treatment – along with the dessert he introduced me to.

51 He is a phenomenal Brother and Son.

~

Happy Father's Day to Joel

June 12, 2016

Dear Joel,

Happy Father's Day to you and many more.

I love you so much and I am so proud of you.

You are a good man, a godly man, a fine husband, and an excellent dad. You have been a fantastic provider for your family, and a blessing to Keswick Christian School and your church.

You are a great leader in the world of work. You always give your best. You have such incredible integrity. You teach those you work with to do their job well, give their best and live life with integrity. When they have a problem, you are there to help and give them guidance. You also care about their families. They are blessed to have you as their manager.

I'm so glad to have you as my son. I thank God for you.

Enjoy Father's Day.

I love you very much.

~

Forty-two Wonderful Things about Amy

1. Great wife
2. Fantastic Mom
3. Loving Friend
4. Fabulous Daughter-in-Law
5. Fun to be with
6. Smart
7. Helpful
8. Problem-solver
9. Practical
10. Great teacher for her boys
11. Creator of special books
12. A Christian who lives her faith
13. Great driver
14. Expects the best from her sons
15. A snowman collector
16. A great heart
17. Loves to read
18. A precious Daughter
19. Supportive of her Husband
20. A blessing to Keswick
21. Supportive of her Sons' sports
22. Keeps a spotless house
23. A computer whizz
24. Kind
25. Plans great trips
26. Surprise party - planner expert
27. Beautiful voice
28. Active in her church

29. Liberty University Graduate
30. Loves cruises
31. Loves a certain little 4-legged critter
32. Enjoys Amazing Race
33. Makes the best corn casserole
34. Enjoys games
35. Fantastic photographer
36. Energetic
37. Great with a cellphone
38. Faithful with a daily wakeup call to Virginia
39. Very safe driver
40. Thoughtful
41. Great shopper
42. Can organize anything

~

Dear Chad

Happy Birthday to you.
Happy Birthday to you.
Happy Birthday dear Chad.
Happy Birthday to you.

I can't believe you are 22 years old. I remember the day you were born. I heard your first cry. I saw you for the first time, when your Dad carried you from your Mother's room to the newborn nursery. I remember when you came home from the hospital and I got to hold you and even take you on a walk around the block. I knew right from the start, you were God's gift to me. I have always loved you and I always will.

I remember Saturday nights when you (and later your Brothers) came over and your Mom and Dad had a 'date night'. I loved rocking you until you fell asleep. I rocked you until you were 7 years - old and the only reason I stopped, was because I couldn't get out of the rocking chair with you in my arms.

So many special memories:
New Year's Eve beating pots and pans at 8 p.m. out on the porch, wishing the neighbors "Happy New Year" and heading off to bed.

Prayers at bedtime.

Sitting reading stories together and talking. I remember the first time you read a book to me.

FAMILY MEMORIES

Your Baptism.

Birthdays with treasure hunts and races and games.

Your years at Keswick: sports, Grandparents' Day and going to your classes with you.

Special programs.

Walking up to Grandpa one day and saying, "Hello fellow diabetic."

Walking up to Grandpa another day and saying, "Hello fellow pastor."

Walking the Mall and touching every outside door.

You and your Alfredo.

Your graduation.

College.

Getting engaged to Chelsea.

There are so many more memories but right now I am looking ahead to:

Your graduation from Liberty.

Your marriage.

Seminary.

AND

The plans God has for your life. You have always held fast to your call to be a Pastor. You are a fantastic young man. You have a heart for God and for people. I love you very much. You will always be in my thoughts and prayers and always on my heart.

Thanks for these memories and so many, many, more. Happy Birthday.

~

A Message from Chad

1/6/2016

Moving to Houston. It's so strange to think that after nearly 22 years of calling Pinellas County my home on earth, that it's over in a week. I have an amazing family I'm leaving behind who've supported my every step in my call to ministry. My mom and dad have made sure to set a good example in treating others with respect and loving humbly, and in how to follow Christ.

My brothers and I haven't always gotten along, but I've learned from them and with them how to still be friends even after major disputes and to have each other's back when the world turns on your family. My extended family has shown me how to love each person you come into contact with, no matter your differences.

I leave friends I've had since preschool, guys I've grown up with in stature and in character. Guys I know will have my back and whose backs I will have should any of us be beaten down by life's circumstances. We will always be friends no matter where life may take us.

I leave behind a church family in Seminole First Baptist who I've gotten to know for only a short time, but who I cherish knowing. Memories of Passion Conference, World Changers, and the many different activities I've gotten to participate in will stick with me, and I have some good friends for life and family for eternity in that church community. But God is good in His leading, and I feel completely at peace in this next step.

God has opened a door in Houston, and I know He will be with me. I have a great church family I will be joining at Nassau Bay Baptist, and I'm excited for what God is already doing and what He will do in and through us! I'm excited for what is to come, both now and even more so when my fiancé will join me this summer as my wife, for I know God has a plan for us!

As Joshua 1:9 commands, first to Joshua, but also to His people now, "Have I not commanded you? Be strong and courageous. Do not be frightened, and do not be dismayed, for the Lord your God is with you wherever you go."

I will go boldly in following, and I ask for your prayers as I follow into this next great adventure.

~

Words of Wisdom from Chad

This happened in the last part of first grade. Chad had finished a test and without thinking, he said something to his friend. His teacher said, "Chad, pull your card." Chad pulled his card and was unusually quiet for the rest of the day. He had never had to pull his card before but he knew what it meant. At the end of the day, he would get no star and no piece of candy. That was the rule.

The end of the day finally came. Chad (our young philosopher) raised his hand. When the teacher recognized him, he said very seriously. "I know I had to pull my card, I know I'm not getting a star, and I know I am not getting a piece of candy, but I am still alive and it's ok."

First You Get Old

When Chad was about five years old, his Great Grandfather Fannin died. Chad went with his Mom and Dad to the funeral. A few days later Chad said to his Aunt Marci, "First you get old, then you get ugly, and then you die."

A week or two later Chad and his Mom Amy came by the house. Joel, his Dad, had been helping us cut a tree down and do some yard work. I was sweaty, covered with dirt, and had no makeup on. As Chad got out of the car and saw me, he got a shocked look on his face. Later I called Marci to let her know I was old and now I had reached the ugly stage". After that when Chad came over to the house he would sit close to me and gently pat my arm

~

Eighteen Wonderful Things about Zach

1. You are very kind and thoughtful.
2. You have a great smile.
3. Little children love you; so does everyone else.
4. You give your best in everything you do.
5. You've never met a stranger.
6. You are your own wonderful self.
7. You gave me a great nickname that makes me smile!
8. Your willingness to do the boring work of transferring our CDs to the IPad means we now have music wherever we go.
9. You have tremendous integrity – your actions are always in line with your values and beliefs.
10. You are a versatile baseball player – giving your best at any position where the manager needs you.
11. You are funny – you tell great jokes.
12. You are a faithful teammate – doing everything that needs to be done without complaining – like cleaning the baseball field after the game.
13. You are the only bowler I know who has reached a ball speed of 30 MPH.
14. You are a great story-teller.
15. You are adventurous – ready to go on a moment's notice.
16. You are a caring grandson.
17. You are confident enough to be silly and playful.
18. You put the "A" in athlete.

~

Words of the Day from Zach

Why is it so easy?

Why is it so easy to pick on someone but not to stand up for them?

Why is it so easy to watch someone sit alone at lunch but not go out of your way to sit with them?

Why is it so easy to stay up late and watch TV or movies but not to wake up early to read your Bible?

Why is it so easy to feel bad for someone but not care enough to talk to them and tell them you care?

Why is it so easy to read this and be convicted but do nothing about it?

Why is it so easy?

Every person you know is a part of your life for one of two reasons:

1. So they can make a difference in your life

Or

2. You can make a difference in their life

A Bible that is falling apart is probably owned be someone whose whole life isn't.

You may only get one chance to make an impact in someone's life, you better take it.

Why don't we begin to look at people through God's eyes Jesus didn't see people as prostitutes and thieves, He saw them all as His children that He loves with all His ability

Thank you for these words, and so many more, that you have written and shared.

~

Dear Clayton

Thank you for all the wonderful memories I have with you in my life. They are in no special order on this list. Memories are like that. They come and they go and they make you smile. Are you ready?

Having you here on Saturday nights and when your Mom and Dad were on a trip.

Rocking you, giving you your bottle and tucking you away.

Saying night time prayers with you

Reading stories

Playing with toys

Finding pictures in the clouds

Celebrating Birthdays

Having treasure hunts

Working puzzles. You are the puzzle champ

Playing games: you even let me win once in a while

Watching TV together

Monk

The Office

Parks and Recreation

Grandparents Day. You are so smart

Sitting in the stands watching you play sports. You made me a soccer fan

Concerts when you played an instrument.

Concerts when you sang. I could always hear your voice.

Listening to you play the guitar and sing. Thanks for playing and singing songs you knew were my favorites. I was amazed how you had taught yourself to play and to print the music off the computer.

Musicals you were in.

Sitting by you in church

Celebrating Christmas

Celebrating New Year's Eve banging pot and pans together on the porch and yelling Happy New Years before your 8 p.m. bedtime.

You stretched out on the couch, with your feet in my lap, both of us watching TV and you getting a foot rub

Caramel syrup and vanilla ice cream "soup"

Trips to village Inn with you and your family after games.

Watching you run track.

Seeing pictures of you and a certain very pretty young lady on your way to your senior prom.

Thanks too, for all the doors you have opened for me to go in and out. You are so thoughtful and you made me feel so special

~

Dear Joel, Amy, Chad, Zach, & Clayton

Happy New Year

May it be a very special year for each of you.

This has been a very special Christmas for me, and I thank you for all you have done to make it so memorable.

Thanks for cookie baking night at the house. Amy, your cookies made with marshmallows, peanuts, cereal and white chocolate were incredible. That day would have been Dad's and my 60th wedding anniversary. That's why I think the cookie party was held that day/night. I think you kids did not want me to be alone. I have a very special family. I love Dad and I miss him very much. It is hard to lose the love of your life. The front door opens many times, but it is never Dad. Thank you for your thoughtfulness.

I had a great time on the cruise. Thanks for making the trip possible. My very favorite time was sitting around the table with the whole gang. It was so precious to me to watch and listen as you interacted with one another; your faces, your laughter, and your talking. Maybe it is a "mom thing," but I loved it.

Had some quiet time sitting out on the balcony and watching the waves and listening to the sound. That was nice.

I enjoyed the sleeping arrangements. I haven't slept in a bunk bed since Marvin was a little one. After he was put in that brace to straighten his hips and legs, he couldn't sleep in his crib. The bunk bed was the answer and I slept with him until he was used to it. That first night on the ship we might have set a new or first time ever record: three grandsons, ages 17 -21, and one 81-year-old grandma sharing two sets of bunk beds. I loved it. Having times with the boys (even when asleep) is always fun. Zach, I'm glad you were able to move to the couch. You were longer than the bunk bed; not good.

Thanks Chad, Zach and Clayton for helping me get around the ship when it was rocking and rolling. You also were great on elevator control and got me to the right floor and the right place at the right time.

Loved being at Ponchos. The fun at the table, the food, and the music was wonderful.

Thanks for the shopping trip, Joel. The two shirts and the bracelet are lovely. Thanks for that special time with you.

Amy, thanks for the pictures of Clayton's senior year. The time has passed so quickly. Soon there will be no more sports, musicals, choir, and Grandparents Day. All will be gone but the memories live on. Aren't you glad memory is part of God's plan for us?

Thanks, too for your gift, the Lava Seat. Most folks don't like to be on the hot seat but I am looking forward to it. Come on winter. Come on sports.

I'm prepared, thanks to you.

Thanks for a very Merry Christmas and memories to cherish the rest of my life.

I love you.

Mom and Grandma

~

Night-Night Time in the Forest

I have sung this song to each of you Children and Grand-children as babies. Only the name has changed as each of you was born. I thank my friend Linda Aldridge for writing the music down on paper for me.

When it's night-night time in the forest

And the birds have gone to bed.

It's night-night time at our house

And Mark must lower his head.

When it's night-night time in the forest

And the birds have lowered their heads

It's night-night time at our house

And Mark must go to bed.

Night, night Mark

Night, night Mark

Night, night, Mark

It's time to go to bed.

* All 5 of you say I never sang this part

Birthdays

Every Birthday was special for Chad, Zach and Clayton. They had a birthday at home but they also had one with Marvin and Phong and Marci and Pam and Grandpa and Grandma. You never knew what was planned. You did know, you would not be handed a pretty wrapped package to open. There would be a challenge. Sometime, it was a treasure hunt, sometime a scavenger hunt, or an amazing Race. Once, it meant climbing to the top of a tree (safety gear on) to find the clue to your gift. One year the treasure hunt was done by boat. Another year, the birthday guy was given safety glasses, a huge bucket of hardened cement and a mallet to break it up. The clue was in a small film holder in the middle of the cement. Imagine planning unusual birthdays over the years for the boys (Chad is nearly 23, Zach is 21 and Clayton is 19) As the boys grew older and the plans became more involved, we worked in teams. Here are two of the games we used in later years. Many thanks to Marvin and Marci for their great ideas. In the younger years of the boys, there were inside or around the yard, and in the park treasure hunts, and quizzes that if you knew the right answers, it helped you to find your treasure. Lots of fun for all of us and great memories forever.

~

Amazing Race

Instructions

Give welcome!
Introduce the Amazing Race.
Take time to look through the bags.
Head out.

Rules of the Race

1. Stay within the speed limit.

2. Be extra careful getting in and out of the car/Sue

3. Always go into stores together. No team member goes any place alone.

4. Have lots of fun. Good Luck!

5. If you need assistance call (phone #) or (phone #)

~~~

The 7-11 on Park Street sells hot dogs. Buy a small one. You must eat all the hotdog before driving away or eat a bite and sit five minutes (after eating the bite) before you drive away.

What is the special of the day at Sonny's?

Take a ride on the overpass near Tyrone Square. Look for the big billboard. What does it advertise?

Run to the end of the pier at Jungle Prada and hit the ball with the paddle ten times

Go to Best Buy and write down the price of a WII Fit with balance board.

Go to Borders. Find the book *Burning Up With the Jonas Brothers*. On page 51 one of the Brothers talks about his musical influences. Which Brother is it? And who are his three musical influences? Get your picture taken with the book.

Be an entertainer at 7655 31st Avenue North. Put on your glasses and red nose. Go to the door and sing "For he's a Jolly Good Fellow." The person listening to you must applaud you before you leave and sign your note pad using your special pencil. You can't verbally ask for applause. You have to find a way to let them know to applaud you. Get your picture taken.

Get a takeout menu from Feola's on 5th Avenue by the trail. Thank the person and give him/her a slinky.

Cold Stone Creamery makes a lot of yummy ice cream concoctions. What are the ingredients in the "Founder's Favorite"?

Go to the Dollar Store near Walmart and buy a puzzle book (example: crossword, Soduko).

Go to Azalea Park, hit the baseball, run around the bases and yell "homerun" as you across home plate. Find the bridge you played on when you were little. Get on it, Juggle three balls for one minute and go down the slide.

Go to Taco Bell on 66th Street and ask the person at the cash register for a free piece of candy.

When you have done everything on the list, go to 1280 66th Street North. Locate the men waving their arms. Step on the red magic mat and report in. The first team there wins the prize.

~

Digital Scavenger Hunt

Clayton's 17th Birthday as Planned by Marvin

Rules for Your Digital Scavenger Hunt

1.Each photo must be shot in selfie style and show all members of the team with object.

2. Objects do not have to be shot in order except the last item must be shot last.

3. You can use your phone to get info but cannot photograph on your phone as a scavenged picture.

4. Before you start, each member of your team must recite and video record the "I'm A Moore" Ballad. (You can practice it for a few minutes) each mistake will receive 30 second penalty.

5. This is a timed event Break no seed limits or any laws. Any item missed or not including all your team members will receive a time penalty.

I'M A Moore
No sky is too high, no sea to rough
Ain't nothing I can't do
Anything in your life worth doing is worth over doing
I'm a fast thinking, rootin tootin, boot scoot-in
often pooting, God fearing son of a gun
Survived the "Carousel of Grizzly Death" with my brother
I've held a live chick in my hand, that thought I was its mother
Going to go around the world twice and talk to everyone once.
Been a lot of lessons in my life

Never drink a large milk shake with a small stomach
Be careful opening gifts from your uncle
Been there done that and going back for more
I'm a fighter, I'm a lover
I'm a Moore

The Digital Scavenger Hunt

1. Framed picture of fishes
2. Likeness of Abraham Lincoln's head
3. Small dog
4. Venus De Aries
5. Giant asterisk symbol
6. Shields Moore's grave marker
7. House sized ice cream cone
8. Lake
9. Airplane
10. George Washington's picture
11. The temperature displayed on Treasure Island Fun Center
12. The Deal or No Deal video game

~

The End

As I write *THE END*, I realize it is only the end of this book...not the end of memories.

In fact, as I wrote these memories, more memories flooded through my mind: old friends, places I have lived, pets, and unexpected adventures.

Some of my family and friends are gone, but the memories we made together, live on to be remembered and enjoyed again and again. I was sitting in church Sunday and the man in front of me was sitting with his arm around his wife's shoulder. That is the way my husband and I sat in church together every Sunday. A warm feeling came over me and a beautiful memory filled my heart

You might be thinking, what about the bad memories: things you wish you had done, things you wish you had said. I had one. The last months of my husband's life, he sat on the porch in his favorite rocking chair. I did the things that needed doing in the house, took care of the yard and brought him what he needed. I wish I had let the 'stuff' go and gone out on the porch, pulled a chair up close, maybe put my head on his shoulder and talked about the places we had lived, his ministry, whatever. He didn't talk much but I could have.

After he died, what I hadn't done made me sad. I couldn't go back and change that, but I did share my experience with a woman whose husband was ill. She began sitting by her husband with her head on his shoulder and talking about the adventures they had together. After her husband died, it was the memories of those last days together that made it easier.

I hope as you have read *Treasures from the Attic of the Heart*, you have begun your own journey as I suggested in the Introduction. Write your memories down. Share them with your friends and family.

Father God, thank you again for your beautiful gift of memory.

~

About the Author

Susan Moore is a Floridian, born in Tampa and graduated from Mound Park School of Nursing in St. Petersburg. After graduation, she married Shields Moore and they moved Louisiana to attend New Orleans Baptist Theological Seminary. After graduation, Shields pastored churches in Virginia until his parents became ill and needed family nearby.

In Tampa Susan served as a nurse at the clinic at the University of South Florida. Shields worked for the City of Tampa and volunteered as the first volunteer chaplain for the fire department. In 1970, he and Susan and their five children moved to St. Petersburg. Shields worked for the Commission on Community Relations and later for the Airport Limo Company. Susan worked a few years in home-health nursing followed by twenty-one years in the Division of Nursing at St. Petersburg Junior College. She is the author of *Nursing Math Simplified*.

When she retired in January 1998, she joined her husband at Tampa International Airport as a volunteer chaplain. Shields had begun this work there in the mid-nineties. He and Susan served together until he became ill. Following his death in April 2012, she retuned one day a week to the Airport Chaplaincy her husband had loved so much.

~

Made in the USA
Columbia, SC
06 May 2018